Illusions

Based on the Thames television series, here is the fascinating story of magic and mystery, conjuring and illusion through the ages, with tales of the great magicians.

And, for the beginner in magic, there are step-by-step instructions for performing conjuring tricks of your own.

You can be a magician too!

Illusions

Fergus Roy and Val Andrews

A Thames Magnet Book

First published 1985 by Methuen Children's Books Ltd
11 New Fetter Lane, London EC4P 4EE
in association with Thames Television International Ltd
149 Tottenham Court Road, London WIP 9LL
Text copyright © 1985 Fergus Roy and Val Andrews
Photographic illustrations copyright © 1985 The Davenport Collection
Line illustrations copyright © 1985 Joanna Quinn
Reproduced, printed and bound in Great Britain by
Hazell Watson & Viney Limited,
Member of the BPCC Group,
Aylesbury, Bucks

ISBN 0 423 01300 9

Contents

About the authors

Fergus Roy

Fergus Roy graduated from Strathclyde University in 1962 in Applied Science and began a career in International Marketing which took him all over the world and included some years in the Far East, where he learned much about classical Chinese magic. His interest in magic, regarded as the most scientific of the Arts, was further stimulated by his marriage to Betty Davenport, the granddaughter of a world-renowned magician and herself an authority on things magical. This finally led him to abandoning his position as a divisional director with Fisons in 1980 in order to devote himself fully to expanding his interest in magical research and in collating the huge family collection of magical memorabilia. This collection is regarded as the greatest of its kind in the world today and his election as a member of the Magic Circle was in recognition of his work in detailing some two thousand books on magic in a complete cross-referenced work, the first of its kind. He devised the television series *Illusions* and is currently working on a number of major projects designed to support the revival of magic and illusion in the United Kingdom.

Val Andrews

Born on 15 February 1926 in Brighton, Sussex, Val became interested in magic at the age of seven through following an elephant, which was destined to be vanished by The Great Carmo. A year later he gave his first show, and turned professional at the age of twelve. He became a variety act, playing theatres all over Great Britain, with London as his permanent base. He appeared at the Stage Door Canteen with Fred Astaire and

Bing Crosby. Later he broadened his activities to include the writing of TV and radio scripts for famous comedians and magicians. Between these activities he has 'grafted' magic in stores and arcades, and written over a hundred books of material for magicians and ventriloquists. During the past few years he has concentrated on the production of his now famous series of biographies of the great men of magic: *Murray*, *Goodnight Mr Dante*, *A Gift From the Gods* (the story of Chung-Ling-Soo), and *Life*, *Dull It Ain't* (the amazing life-story of Horace Goldin). Today, Val alternates his writing work with the performance of his one-man lecture entertainment, *Magic and Memories*.

Preface

During a break in televising one of the programmes in the series *Illusions* several of the camera and set crew gathered round and began asking me to tell them more about the famous magicians I had been talking about. I sat on the edge of the set desk and talked well into our lunch break about some of the great magicians of the past and their quite extraordinary adventures. It was during one of these sessions that one cameraman said, 'Why don't you write these stories down?'

I had never thought of doing this and with mixed feelings of fear and enthusiasm agreed to try and set out what I felt were some of the stories which I like best. I could see that the main obstacle to accomplishing this was not which stories to include but which to leave out. To give you some idea of the monumental task you must appreciate that the history of magic began with the dawn of time, through the Pharaohs, some five thousand years ago. Then I had to give heed to the Davenport collection of which I am custodian and which contains in three store houses over seventy-five tons of magical memorabilia including thirty-five tons of paper! There are over five thousand books and pamphlets on magic alone, never mind the vast quantity of posters, letters, documents, photographs, magical props and the collected knowledge that a family which has been steeped in magic for nearly a century accumulates in that time. After a number of sleepless nights I suddenly remembered that some of the most interesting books ever written on magicians of the past and which had always stimulated my interest were written by a fine English magician and author who was also a good friend, Val Andrews.

We determined that the object of the book would not only be to make some of these famous magicians come to life again in print but also to include a number of easy-to-do magic tricks which might just start a youngster today on a hobby leading to the fame and fortune of some of the magicians of the past. What you will find is that while many of the tricks described all seem easy to do and your reaction may be the same as most people when they learn a magical secret, 'Oh that's obvious', let me assure you it isn't. I have spent some wonderful evenings entertaining friends with the simplest tricks, which they ask me to perform time and time again, for I never – and I mean never ever – tell them how the trick is done. I would add that whoever reads this book must not be put off by thinking what age they should start. Of course many magicians start at a very early age but some of the most famous began when they were in their late forties or even fifties!

Let me now just tell you a little about the Davenport collection and how it all began.

In 1897 a boy called Lewis Davenport, who was only fourteen years of age, stood outside Hamley's in Regent Street and was deeply impressed by the variety of tricks and magical effects he saw in the window. Hamley's was at that time one of the largest magical emporia, as they were called, in London and indeed the world. This youngster was no ordinary boy, for already at that tender age he was a professional magician and juggler. He determined that he would start his own company and the next year he established L. Davenport & Co., in the East End of London, little knowing that he would become a legend, and that he would own one of the largest magical shops in the world.

The famous collection began by accident. By 1911 Lewis Davenport had become very well known both at home and internationally as a magician and his business was thriving. His passion was to maintain magical secrets, and every time any magical items came onto the market he would buy them and put them, lock stock and barrel, into store. By 1920 the amount of material was so great that he had to rent the crypt of Holy Trinity Church in Kingsway, London, an almost perfect tomb, to house the collection.

His zeal for preserving magical secrets was continued by his son George Davenport, known as Gilly, and then by his granddaughter Betty. By 1980 this now massive collection, well in excess of 150 tons, was out of control. It had not really been sorted or organised. It had been packed away, layer upon layer, into the crypt and due to the sheer weight of the material much damage had been done. Some stocks were nearly twenty-five feet high! A decision with regard to its future was made during a momentous meeting of the company in February 1980. Three possibilities for the collection's future were discussed.

First, that it could be sold in one huge auction. This was discarded as the whole purpose of the collection had been to preserve the secrets. Second, that it could be taken out and burned in order to keep the secrets. This was discussed at length and was very much the front runner for some time. However, a third suggestion was that the collection be sorted out and the great illusions brought back to working condition and shown to the public again after a lapse of some fifty years. Some form of National Museum of Magic was then discussed where the magnificent collection of posters and magical material could be shown to the public in parallel with an exhibition, and it was this final suggestion that prompted me, after some soul-searching, to start the mammoth task of sorting the collection out.

This took two years and over forty tons of broken and damaged items were thrown out onto the scrap heap. Finally the job was done and a clear idea of the hard core of the collection could at last be perceived. It was a veritable treasure. Examples of almost every famous magician's illusion acts, countless documents, records from the meticulous files of the many companies purchased by Davenport's, artefacts and memorabilia revealed that the collection was far more import-ant than had ever been thought possible.

Now it had been sorted the next step was natural: show these wonderful illusions to the public and talk about the incredible stories revealed in the manuscripts. Thames Television was approached, and to the delight of Davenport's were equally enthusiastic about the idea. And so a television series was born.

I wonder now what that young lad outside Hamley's would have thought then if he had guessed what he was about to start when he walked away from that famous store determined to start his own business. I would like to think he would have approved wholeheartedly, as he loved magic, he loved entertaining people, he loved illusion and I believe he would have enjoyed *Illusions* as a concept for the show is a tribute to him and his generation for what they have left us in terms of mystery, entertainment and spectacle.

All the proceeds from this book are being given to a new group, specially formed to establish a permanent home for the collection, and all of us at Davenport's look forward to the day when the collection will be put on view and the wonders of the ages placed before a generation who never knew the magical legends of the past.

Fergus Roy 1984

Fig. 1. **Louis Davenport** (1882–1960)
Founder of the Davenport Collection of magic and illusions.

Chapter 1
A brief history of illusion

Today we can watch the world's greatest magicians from the comfort of a favourite armchair, through that magic which we all tend to take for granted . . . television. This was not always so, for our fathers and grandfathers had to go to the theatre, or some other form of live entertainment, in order to enjoy the same experience. The theatre has a long history, but magic has a longer one. Where, when, and how did it all begin? In this first chapter we will try to reconstruct the history of illusion as a form of entertainment.

Historians can take us back to the pyramids of Egypt for the first records of magic. But I would venture to trace the conjurer back almost as far as the existence of man himself. The desire to fool one's friends is instinctive: how often have you seen a toddler hide a favourite toy in order to rejoice over its reappearance? This desire to hide and later retrieve objects can even be seen in animals. But some prehistoric men took it all further and discovered that they could gain respect from their fellows with primitive deceptions of the 'which hand is it in' type.

So much for theory; let us examine facts. Scientific study of remains has shown us that the witch-doctors of Africa appeared a great deal earlier than did the priests of the Egyptian temples. There can be little doubt that the witch-doctors were conjurers as well as herbalists, using all their talents to play upon the superstitions of the people. A typical device of the witch-doctor was the holding of a cowrie shell in front of each of a number of suspects in turn, and when blood mysteriously spouted from the shell, the guilty party had been found. Needless to say, the flow of blood from the shell was caused by mechanical means, entirely under the control of the witch-doctor. The principle upon which this ancient deception was based was used by the French magician, Robert-Houdin, in the mid nineteenth century for his 'Inexhaustible Bottle', in which he poured an enormous number of completely different beverages from a single bottle. So we find that a trick which we could be forgiven for thinking no more than 150 years old, originated in fact many thousands of years ago.

So we have found our first professional magicians in the witch-doctors of Africa, where man is longest established. Their counterparts would eventually appear in Asia, Europe and Australia, where Aboriginal magicians also held court. These original inhabitants of Australia invented the boomerang, which has a magic all of its own.

The first written accounts of magical exploits are found on early Egyptian papyrus. Some of these record feats of magic which read like miracles. One of these was performed by Jajemenekh who caused the waters of a lake to part, at least two thousand years before Moses performed a similar act with the waters of the Red Sea. Earlier still, another Egyptian wonder-worker, Weba-aner, had transformed a small model of a crocodile into a large, living reptile of that species. Sophisticated sorcerers were these Egyptian magicians, who had taken the old witch-doctors' ideas and elaborated on them so that they could astound and influence the Pharaohs. The descriptions of many of their achievements have obviously been exaggerated in the papyrus and in translation. Yet some of the feats described can be recognised as being both practical and possible, and in some cases the inspiration for the modern magician's tricks. For example, Cheops, who was the builder of the great pyramid at Gizeh, had a favourite magician, Dedi, who performed feats of decapitation. It is recorded that he severed the head of a goose and, after having placed the head and body at a considerable distance apart, restored it. During the first half of the nineteenth century an Italian conjurer, Bartolomeo Bosco, took the trick a stage further when he beheaded two pigeons, a black and a white, only to restore the heads to the wrong bodies! The trick was thought to be too gruesome for modern audiences and therefore hardly ever seen during the last hundred years. Yet in 1960 I saw the Italian magician Chefalo perform it. He presented it with such delicacy that no offence was given to the audience. They felt sure that such a charming man would not really hurt the birds (which indeed he did not).

2

We can find the beginnings of theatrical magic in the performances of the yogis and fakirs of India, even if the sun was their spotlight and the sky their backcloth. Wandering Indian conjurers were performing, in return for a few coins from the crowd, before the Saxons came to Britain or the Moors invaded Spain. Most of them would appear to have performed the same feats. The cutting and restoring of a turban, the catching of coins out of thin air, causing a toy duck to sink and reappear at command in a tub of water. They would cause a small object, such as a pebble or berry, to disappear from beneath a shallow cup, only to reappear under another. Three of these feats are regularly performed today, even if the modern conjurer is more likely to cut and restore a length of soft white rope, than a turban. But the collection of coinage from nowhere has passed into the twentieth-century magician's repertoire almost unchanged, as has the trick with the three cups.

Indeed, the three cups and balls is probably the most enduring and universally performed trick. Right through the ages, by witch-doctors with shells and bones, by fakirs with cups and berries, everywhere and ever the plot is the same: a small object is transposed from cup to cup, or shell to shell, or bowl to bowl. The object is made to penetrate through the vessel, and in many versions of the trick larger objects, such as fruit or bread rolls, are produced from beneath each cup by way of finale. Perhaps the most skilled and renowned performers with the cups have been the 'galli-galli' boys of North Africa. The earliest Europeans to visit those parts returned with stories of their feats. In the North African version the climax is to produce a live baby chick from each cup.

By the Middle Ages, European conjurers were performing with the cups as well as catching coins and cutting and restoring ropes in market places and fairs. There can be little doubt that Crusaders had brought some of the feats of native conjurers back to Europe. Of course there had been 'wizards' in Europe long before that time. Merlin and less well-remembered wizards had often prospered through the superstitions of the people. But they were astrologers and herbalists, men who claimed supernatural powers. Their secrets were passed from father to son or master to servant. Their only likeness to the true conjurers would be that the conjurer sometimes appeared robed

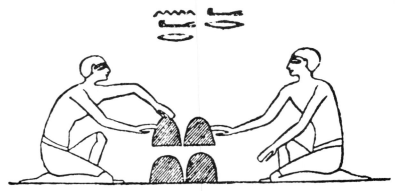

Fig. 2. The earliest version of the cups and balls trick from the burial chamber of the Beni Hassan tomb in Egypt (c. 2500 BC)

like a wizard. We are fortunate in knowing quite a good deal about these performing magicians of the Middle Ages, not so much from the written word as from contemporary artists' impressions.

Students of the Tarot assure us that although they cannot trace the designs used on today's cards further back than the late fourteenth century, they seem to be based on much earlier pictures. This would certainly appear to be so with the style of the 'Bateleur' or 'Juggler' who, as drawn, is quite obviously a conjurer. On his table rest coins, dice, thimbles, cups and a knife out of its sheath. There is also a purse, from which a handkerchief protrudes. In his left hand is a wand, and in his right a coin. From his manner of holding these he would seem to be about to make the coin vanish. The pilgrim-style hat which he wears is in the form of a figure eight, regarded as a symbol of eternity.

Drawings and paintings from Elizabethan and Stuart times reveal much about the conjurers who entertained at fairs. Usually the conjurer is depicted as working from behind a small table, and the same items of equipment are invariably illustrated: cups, balls, wand or rod, and frequently a fowl which, due to the primitive style of drawing, could be either the real or the imitation kind. Sometimes he is depicted wearing an apron with a large pocket, rather like the apron worn by a modern carpenter.

The biggest change in the world of illusion came when the conjurer ceased to be a busker, working for whatever he could collect, and performed in a place where people paid to enter and see his wonders. At first it would have been a fairground tent or booth. Such a magician was Isaac Fawkes, who is captured for us in Hogarth's famous engraving, 'Southwark Fair'. Hogarth shows us Fawkes standing in front of his booth, trying to persuade the people to enter. Another engraving, by Sutton Nichols, shows Fawkes in performance, producing eggs from a large bag. He appears in the engravings as a plump-faced man, well-dressed and wearing the powdered wig of the period. His repertoire included tricks with mice, money and live birds. He also had an apple tree which blossomed and bore fruit in less than a minute! This and other mechanical wonders were made for him by Christopher Pinchbeck, a Fleet Street clockmaker. When Fawkes died in 1731 he left ten thousand pounds, which was at that time a fortune.

One of the first magicians in Britain to perform in theatres and halls was John Henry Anderson, the self-styled Wizard of the North. He was born in Aberdeen on 15 July 1814. In his youth he played in fairground booths, but soon decided to come in out of the cold, hiring salons and theatres to bring his show to the attention of a new audience, the kind that did not frequent fairgrounds. He had some wonderful tricks and illusions. He poured any drink called for from a magic bottle, produced flowers at his fingertips, conjured a young boy from a simple portfolio, and then caused that child to float in mid-air. Anderson caught bullets, fired at him from a pistol, in his teeth, made live doves appear from a cooking-pot and produced a boiling pudding from a borrowed hat. Little wonder that Queen Victoria, who was fond of such entertainments, summoned him to appear before her at Balmoral in 1849. He made a tour of America in 1861, but while in the southern states was forced to drop his Wizard of the North title, for diplomatic reasons. Anderson was the first of the great magical showmen who knew the value of publicity. Wherever he played he would issue free butter-moulds to the dairy, so that all the local people could read his name at their breakfast tables. He stencilled his name on pavements and distributed booklets giving details of his career and travels. He died in Darlington, where he

Figs. 3 & 4. **John Henry Anderson** – 'The Wizard of the North'
– Scotland's greatest magician (1814–74).

was currently performing, in 1874, at the age of fifty-nine.

While Anderson was pioneering theatre magic in Britain, the great French wizard, Robert-Houdin was doing the same thing in France. After youthful fairground escapades, Houdin had settled to the watchmaker's trade, which he practised for twenty years. Then, at the age of forty, he decided to return to the activities of his youth and become a professional conjurer. But he really did it with style, creating his own theatre with crystal chandeliers and tasteful decor. He had criticised the conjurers of his day for working with floor-length cloths on their tables, and for wearing long robes. He, Houdin, would work in a simple tailcoat, with his apparatus standing on graceful, undraped pedestals. He was as good as his word, and his *Soirées Fantastiques* opened in Paris in July 1845. He performed all the feats presented by Anderson, and also an orange tree which blossomed and bore fruit, circled by mechanical butterflies! His presentation of the levitation feat was given a novel twist. He implied not only that mesmerism had a lot to do with it, but also that the newly discovered ether, used in surgical operations, was involved. In Paris the Musée Grevin still exhibits a waxwork of Houdin, levitating his young son. Upstairs in the same building, a small theatre where the magician actually performed continues to be known as the 'Salle de Robert-Houdin'.

Houdin wrote several books. His memoirs, full of adventures which may or may not have happened, included an account of his part in quelling a North African uprising. His *Secrets* are still read with interest by the modern magicians.

There had been magical textbooks before, the most important being *The Discoveries of Witchcraft* written by Reginald Scott in 1584. The author had been so horrified to see innocent women put to death for the alleged practice of witchcraft that he had decided to expose the secrets used, and thus show their origin to be natural rather than supernatural. For more than two centuries this book became the basis of many others. Scott had gained his knowledge from a French conjurer, John Cautares. One of the secrets in the book, published four hundred years ago, is that of the cut and restored rope.

But without doubt the first really important magical textbook to be published was *Modern Magic* by Professor Hoffmann. The

Fig. 5. A woodcut frontispiece to Pablo Minguet e Yrol's *Enganos a Ojos Vistos* (1733) – the first Spanish book on deceptions. *Copy from the Davenport Collection.*

Fig. 6. A fifteenth century painting of a sleight-of-hand performer by Hieronymus Bosch. *Photo from the Davenport Collection.*

The diſcouerie
of witchcraft,
Wherein the lewde dealing of witches
and witchmongers is notablie detected, the
knauerie of coniurors, the impietie of inchan-
tors, the follie of ſoothſaiers, the impudent falſ-
hood of couſenors, the infidelitie of atheiſts,
the peſtilent practiſes of Pythoniſts, the
curioſitie of figurecaſters, the va-
nitie of dreamers, the begger-
lie art of Alcu-
myſtrie,
The abhomination of idolatrie, the hor-
rible art of poiſoning, the vertue and power of
naturall magike, and all the conueiances
of Legierdemaine and iuggling are deciphered:
and many other things opened, which
haue long lien hidden, howbeit
verie neceſſarie to
be knowne.
Heerevnto is added a treatiſe vpon the
nature and ſubſtance of ſpirits and diuels,
&c: all latelie written
by Reginald Scot
Eſquire.
1. Iohn.4,1.
Beleeue not euerie ſpirit, but trie the ſpirits, whether they are of God; for manie falſe prophets are gone out into the world, &c.
1584
H.p.1202.

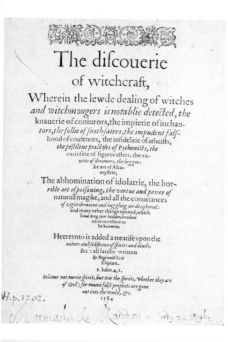

Fig. 7. *The Discovery of Witchcraft* (1584), the first major book in English to reveal how tricks were performed. *From the Davenport Collection.*

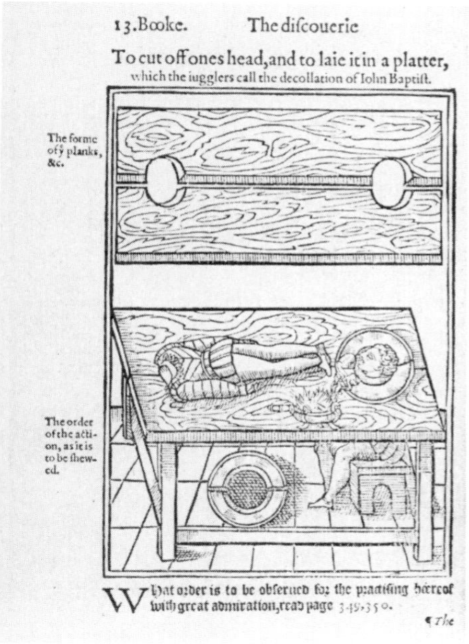

Fig. 8. An illustration from *The Discovery of Witchcraft* showing how an illusion was performed by trickery rather than witchcraft. *From the Davenport Collection.*

Professor was in fact a barrister, Angelo Lewis, and when he published the book in 1875 he had already fallen foul of the professional conjurers for the publication of many of their secrets in the *Boy's Own Paper*. The book was the first to tell the reader 'how to do it' rather than just 'how it was done'. Well written and illustrated, *Modern Magic* is still in print a hundred years or more after its first publication. Hoffmann claimed that he wrote the book so that conjurers, who were, he felt, lacking in originality, would be forced to invent new tricks. Certainly the flow of new tricks and illusions seems to have *Modern Magic* as its source. Since the turn of the century many thousands of books and pamphlets, devoted entirely to magic, have appeared in print. In 1912 Will Goldston, London-based magical dealer and author, produced the most elaborate magical book to appear up to that time. It was titled *Exclusive Magical Secrets* and was handsomely bound in seal roan, with a lock. Many of the secrets as described by Goldston were totally incorrect. He was a great character, with a lively imagination.

Fig. 9. An engraving by Queverdo showing the great **Pinetti** nailing a card to a wall by a pistol shot, from *La Magie Blanche Devoilée*. From the Davenport Collection.

The great days of the stage magician arrived with the music hall and variety shows. The illusionist, particularly, was much in demand to work in big theatres. Just to make it clear, if a feat is performed with a duck, or a ball, or a bottle, it's a trick. But if it's performed with people, it's an illusion.

Typical of the illusionists of the music-hall era was Carl Hertz. Born in San Francisco in 1865, he came to Britain in 1884 with a small act of card magic and a clever bird-cage trick. Due to his pleasant manner and smart showmanship, he made a big success and was soon able to add several illusions to his act. One of these, the 'Vanishing Lady', had been shown here earlier by its inventor, Bautier de Kolta, without making anyone too excited. But in Hertz's hands it was a big success. He would seat the lady in a chair and cover her with a cloth. It was clear to the audience that she was still there, for her form could be detected beneath the material, right up to the moment when Hertz snatched the cloth away, to show that she had vanished. He had another illusion in which a lady escaped from a cross to which she had been chained. There were objections to this, from religious organisations, so Hertz disguised the cross as a tree. But although his illusions made him a star, it was his presentation of the 'Bird-Cage Trick' that got him the most applause. A small cage, containing a live canary, would seem to melt away into thin air when held between his hands. It was widely rumoured that a canary was killed at every performance. This is unlikely to have been true, but the rumour persisted, until in 1921 the magician was summoned to give evidence before a select committee of the House of Commons, who were investigating the treatment of performing animals. Hertz performed the trick with a marked canary and vindicated himself. Years later, after Hertz had died, Will Goldston claimed to have made a special cage for the House of Commons demonstration, quite unlike the one that was in regular use. When Hertz died in 1924, Goldston wrote that 'he had died a disappointed man'. Yet, when one examines his long career, his world tours, and the fact that he was still working regularly at the time he died, one wonders what he was disappointed about!

Dozens of magicians and illusionists appeared in music halls all over London and the rest of Britain. Charles Morrit made a donkey vanish, Gus Fowler filled the stage with magically produced watches and clocks, Sydney Lee threw cards that had been chosen into the gallery of the theatre for verification. Rameses presented illusions in Egyptian setting, Gustave Fasola worked in Indian disguise, Charles Bertram became the first magician to use a catch-phrase ('Isn't it wonderful?'). There were many, many others, but perhaps the outstanding magician of the period was David Devant. He was 'discovered' by J. N. Maskelyne of the famous theatre of mystery in Piccadilly, which bore his name. Maskelyne saw Devant performing at London's Oxford Music Hall. Impressed, he asked Devant if he could invent a new illusion for his theatre. The result was the 'Artist's Dream', in which an artist falls asleep in front of the portrait of his sweetheart that he has been painting. He dreams that she steps out of the picture, which is just what happens in the illusion. Maskelyne liked the 'Artist's Dream' so much that he built a playlet around it, which ran at his theatre for years. It was Devant who persuaded Maskelyne to put the newly invented moving-pictures into his programme in 1896. Later, when Maskelyne's partner Cooke had died, and his own fortunes had declined, it was Devant who modernised the show and saved Maskelyne from bankruptcy. The old showman made Devant a partner, and Maskelyne and Devant's became an institution. To the British public for many years, David Devant was *the* magician. He suffered from paralysis at quite a young age and fought the illness for many years, but by 1922 he was unable any longer to perform. He survived, as a grumpy invalid, until his death in 1941 at the age of seventy-three.

Music hall was an elaboration of the kind of entertainment earlier presented in taverns, and as such was a rather rough affair. But then, at the turn of the century, Sir Oswald Stoll and other music-hall impressarios got the idea of changing the whole character of the entertainment. They took out the tables and the pots of ale, and made the entertainment more suitable for a family audience. This cleaned-up version of music-hall was known as 'variety', and ran for more than fifty years.

Variety shows created more opportunities for magicians and illusionists. The improved stage conditions made for bigger, better magic acts, and of course a family audience was more appreciative. This then was the golden era of the great illusionists: Chung Ling Soo with his elaborate Chinese illusions, the

Figs. 10 & 11. Front-of-house pictures for the illusionist, **Jules Heller** (c. 1920). *From the Davenport Collection.*

Great Lafayette whose quick changes were as astounding as his mysteries, Houdini whom no lock could hold, and a magical 'whirlwind' from America, Horace Goldin.

One of the most elaborate acts of the period was that of Le Roy, Talma, and Bosco. Servais Le Roy was the illusionist, Talma was not only his principal assistant but also a magicienne in her own right, and Bosco was a bearded, bald-headed funny man, who interrupted the other two. The trio featured breath-taking transformations. In one of these, the trio changed places with each other in three small separate cabinets. At the climax, Le Roy would disappear, to return almost immediately in the pit, holding a conductor's baton.

Le Roy was originally from Belgium, but it was in London that he established a supply-house for illusions and scenery. The variety boom lured him back on the stage. He will always

Fig. 12. Poster for **Le Roy, Talma and Bosco** – a brilliant illusionists' act with superb sleight-of-hand. Bosco was the buffoon. *From the Davenport Collection.*

14

Fig. 13. The beautiful **Talma** – a brilliant manipulator of coins. She continued performing for some years after Servais Le Roy retired. *Photo from the Davenport Collection.*

be remembered by magicians as the inventor of 'Asrah, the Floating Princess'. In this, Le Roy would pretend to hypnotise Talma, laying her on a couch, and covering her with a sheet. She would then seem to float, right up into the air. When she had reached about eight feet, Le Roy would pass a large hoop over her draped, floating form. Higher still she floated, until Le Roy could just reach the hem of the sheet with his fingers. Then he would raise a hand to silence the orchestra, and speak the lines which have become traditional with all who present the illusion: 'There she lies, asleep in the air, and there she could remain should I so desire. Yet, behold . . . the impossible!' He would grasp the hem of the sheet and pull, so that it fluttered to the stage. The Princess Asrah had not only floated, but had disappeared into thin air. Magicians had levitated people before; Robert-Houdin had done it half a century before. But none of them had made the person vanish for a climax. It was a big success, but on the first performance Le Roy was so worried

Fig. 14. **Servais Le Roy** performing his amazing illusion: Asrah – The Floating Princess.

LE ROY ★ TALMA ★ BOSCO

LE ROYS INCREDIBLY MARVELLOUS EFFECT.

THE GREATEST LEVITATION MYSTERY EVER SHOWN.

SERVAIS LE ROY

WORLDS MONARCH OF MAGIC

about it that he had Bosco standing by with a comedy trick in case something went wrong.

Variety became more demanding as the years went by. It demanded novelty, and magicians were beginning to realise that laughter was as important as applause. A fine comedy magician was Fred Culpitt, with clever magic and very funny talk. He produced a very tall lady from a tiny dollshouse. Carlton, billed as the Human Hairpin on account of his tall, spare figure, looked about seven feet tall in tights, with a built-up bald head. As he plucked cards out of thin air he would quip: 'This man must get a very large salary per week, per-haps!' and 'Ooh, mother, the conjurer looks like a fountain pen!' His act was ruined when he started to put on weight. Another fine comedy act was that of Frank Van Hoven, an American with several tricks which never worked. Indeed, he would have been out of business if they had. He made two boys from the audience sit on blocks of ice while he attempted to conjure. He was billed as the Man Who Made Ice Famous.

In the twenties and thirties magicians and illusionists had to speed up, competing with the movies, and later the talkies. 'Magical Revue' became the thing, and the best of these was presented by Dante, a Danish-American. He was born Harry August Jansen in Copenhagen in 1884. At the age of six he went to America. (He always used to say that he left Denmark because he didn't seem to be getting anywhere!) His story was a traditional one. First success was with a small act of sleight of hand, then he presented an illusion act, using his five children as assistants and his wife conducting the orchestra in the pit. As The Great Jansen he toured the world with some success. But in the twenties he entered into partnership with the illusionist Howard Thurston, and became a star. Thurston was America's leading illusionist of those days and wanted Jansen to take a duplicate of his show to those parts of America where he did not tour himself. He gave Jansen the name of 'Dante', and titled this version of the show *Sim-Sala-Bim*. But Dante brought the show to Europe instead, and created a sensation with it. It had been a good show to start with, but Dante made it even better. He was a magnetic performer, with great, expressive eyes, a mane of snow-white hair and a Satanic goatee. His smile was infectious, and his light-hearted style made the show move along with a swing. He had a new 'twist' on all the old mysteries. In *Fun in a Barber's Shop* Dante played the part of the barber, and put on a white coat and a carnival head. The show's comedian sat in the chair, draped with a sheet, and likewise dressed in a carnival head. When Dante had finished shaving the comedian, the funny fellow would rise from the chair, remove the carnival head and prove to be Dante. The barber turned out to be the comic! In 'Backstage' he turned the whole theatre round, and worked facing a backcloth with an audience painted on it. The real audience thought they saw how the tricks were done, but Dante fooled them! During a two-hour show, the audience saw twenty full-stage illusions, each in a different setting, and twice that number of small tricks and surprises. In 1947 Dante made a final tour of Great Britain, with a rather smaller show. But the audience still got more than their money's worth. He co-starred with Laurel and Hardy in a movie, *A Haunting We Will Go*, in which the boys hired as assistants, all but wreck the show. He died of a heart attack at his ranch in California on 16 June 1955, soon after he had spread the properties from his show out on a meadow to be destroyed by the elements. I have never seen a magician to equal Dante. He was truly the final figure in a parade of giants. Magic's golden age lies mouldering on a California meadow.

Variety began to fade during the fifties and expired during the early sixties. Although magicians continued to be seen in cabaret and at children's parties, magic declined as a profession.

Television created its own magical stars, such as Robert Harbin whose 'Zig-Zag-Lady', in which his lady assistant's middle was moved, became the most popular and widely copied illusion in the world. A crazy character called Tommy Cooper managed to make himself into a big television star by his

Fig. 15. The fourth generation of Davenports, Billy & Fergus, practising an illusion before a charity performance.

inspired fumbling of tricks. Yet Tommy Cooper and Robert Harbin were only able to become stars of television through the years of experience that they had gained in variety. Now variety was dead, where were the magical stars of the future to come from?

Throughout the history of show business, as one door has closed another has opened. By the end of the sixties the working-men's clubs had become big business, and a new wave of magicians were finding an outlet for their talents.

During the seventies a 'magic boom' erupted in America, doubtless inspired by television appearances by several fine illusionists: David Copperfield, Doug Henning, Siegfried and Roy. Suddenly a whole nation wanted to participate. Close-up magicians were to be found in bars and cafes, and every cabaret had its illusionist.

In Great Britain the magic craze has followed but, as usual, in a rather quieter way. Here, magic is popular again as an exciting form of entertainment, but even more popular as a participating hobby. And why not? The ability to amuse one's friends with a few intriguing mysteries is a great social asset.

Four magical effects for you to perform

The cut and restored string

This is a good trick that can be easily made from articles found in most homes. The effect is that a string is shown to be threaded through a drinking straw. The straw has had a portion cut away from its centre, so that the middle of the string can be seen. When the straw is bent in half, the centre loop of the string protrudes, and is cut away by the conjurer with scissors. But the straw is straightened again, and the now restored string can be pulled to and fro!

Preparation: You will need one of those rather fat plastic drinking straws; a length of string about two feet long, and another piece about two inches long; a pair of nail scissors and some glue.

To prepare for a performance, cut a portion from the centre of the straw near the centre, being careful to leave at least half the straw centre intact (see Diagram 1). Take the short piece of string and glue it into the aperture as illustrated. When the glue is dry you can thread the longer strong through the straw and you are ready to perform.

Performance: Pull the string to and fro, keeping the open aperture in the straw turned away from the audience. Bend the straw so that the short piece is seen, and cut it, taking care not to cut the longer string. Cut away the false portion as completely as possible. Now straighten the straw, again turning the aperture away from the audience. Get two people to hold onto an end each of the string, and move the straw up and down its length to show its restoration. Finally draw the string from the straw, and show that it is in fact truly restored.

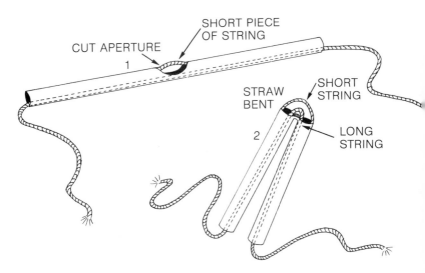

A nice trick, and although not very old, it is based on a principle explained by Reginald Scott in his book *The Discovery of Witchcraft*.

The obedient ball

This is a very simple trick to perform, though quite effective. I have included it because although it is no earth-shattering mystery it is typical of the tricks performed by very early magicians.

A ball is shown to have a cord threaded through a hole in its centre, and a bead at each end of the cord prevents the ball from dropping off. The magician takes one bead in each hand and allows the ball to run down the cord, from top to bottom. Then, reversing his hands he does so again. He repeats this a number of times. Then he allows the ball to run down the cord, and says: 'Stop!' The ball stops, somewhere near the centre of the cord. He says: 'Start!' and it falls to the bottom of the cord.

Preparation: Exactly as already described, except that the hole which has been bored through the ball is not straight, but as illustrated below. You can buy it from most magic shops.

Performance: If the cord is held fairly slackly, the ball will simply fall down its length. But if the cord is tightened, the ball will stop, and fall again when it is slackened. A very simple trick it is true, but it can be built up by having members of the audience tell the ball to stop. Naturally, control is still completely in the magician's hands, and the ball will either stop or not, according to the forcefulness of the command.

Magic with matchboxes

Here are three tricks with matchboxes, all extremely simple, but effective because a matchbox is an article to be found anywhere and the tricks can be seemingly impromptu, even when you have had an opportunity to 'set them up'!

Coin from matchbox

A matchbox lying on the table is partially open, and when it is inverted nothing drops from it, so it is assumed to be empty. The conjurer shuts the box, mutters a magic word, and shakes the box. A sound of an object rattling is heard. The box is reopened, and a coin is discovered inside.

Preparation: The illustration shows how a coin can be wedged between the tray and the box, and with this set-up, the box can be inverted without any danger of the coin falling out.

Performance: Pick up the partly open box, and turn it upside-down, shaking it a little, to make sure that everyone notices that nothing falls out and that no noise is heard. Do not tell them that the box is empty, or they may ask to examine it. Snap the box shut between the forefinger and thumb of one hand. Then shake it, very slowly and gently, so that the coin inside makes no noise. Increase the speed of shaking until the coin is heard. You thus create the illusion of the gradual materialisation of an object. Open the box and drop out the coin. Before your spectators start an inquest, perform the following trick with the same box. . . .

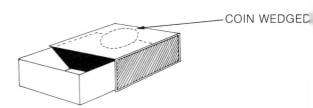

COIN WEDGED

Eerie matchbox

A matchbox is laid on the back of the conjurer's hand. When told to, it rises eerily to stand on its end!

Performance: Have the tray sticking out of the box by a mere fraction of an inch. In placing it on the back of the left hand, shut the box with the fingers of the right hand, trapping some of the loose skin, over the left knuckles, between the tray and the box. Manipulation of the left hand, even a slight movement, will make the box raise itself in eerie fashion. Try it!

Production of matches

A matchbox is shaken, and as there is no rattle it is obviously empty. Yet when opened it is found to be filled with matches. When the box is closed and shaken again they are heard to rattle.

Preparation: Break a small piece from a match, so that it can be wedged in the tray of the box to hold the matches securely, as in the illustration below.

Performance: Pick up the prepared box and shake it. Look disappointed, as if you needed a match. Open the box, with the matches towards you, and away from the audience. Poke an exploring finger into the box, seemingly looking to see what is there, but actually dislodging the wedged match. Show the matches by tilting the tray towards the audience. Close and shake the box, reopen, and extract a match.

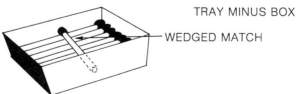

TRAY MINUS BOX

WEDGED MATCH

Do not present this trick as a puzzle. Present it rather as a natural event. You want a match, the box is seemingly empty . . . yet it is full!

Chapter 2
Escapology

What is an escapologist, and how does he differ from a magician? There is of course a great similarity, for they are both in the business of deceiving the public, in the nicest possible way of course. But while the art of the magician is varied, the escapologist has only one basic trick. He is restrained, and he escapes. However, that basic feat can be dressed up in a hundred different ways to give variety to a performance. The escape-artist can be tied with rope, chained and padlocked, handcuffed, restrained with leg-irons, trussed up in a straight-jacket, imprisoned in a packing case or buried alive. Always he will escape . . . well, nearly always.

The best-known escape-artist is Houdini: even with the passing of more than fifty years since his death, he is still a household name. Simple escapes had been performed in market-places and fairgrounds and even as diversions by stage magicians, long before Houdini appeared on the scene. But it took that great performer to popularise escapes as a form of big-time entertainment.

Like so many great performers, Houdini was born to a poor immigrant family who had journeyed to America from Budapest, Hungary. By his own claim he was born in Appleton, Wisconsin, on 6 April 1874. However, there is now good reason to believe that he was actually born on 24 March of the same year, but in Budapest, and brought to America shortly after-wards. Perhaps he wished to be known as an American by birth as well as by nationality. His father was a rabbi of the Jewish faith, who made a poor living translating for other immigrants. The family name was Weiss (or Weisz) and Houdini was named Ehrich. His interest in magic sprang from the discovery of a tattered copy of *The Memoirs of Robert-Houdin* found in a secondhand bookstore. The great French magician became his idol through those pages, and by adding an 'i' to the Frenchman's name he produced 'Houdini' (which literally means 'like Houdin').

This was not the first stage name that he had used, for at the age of nine he had run away from home and performed as an acrobat, calling himself 'Ehrich the Great'. After weeks of wandering he had knocked, tired and hungry, at the door of a Mrs Flitcroft. He explained to her that he was not begging, but would like to give her a performance in exchange for a glass of milk. The good lady watched gravely as he picked up pins with his eyelids. She gave him the milk and a bed for the night and sent him on his way with a bag of home-made pies and cakes. Many years later, when Houdini was famous all over the world, he secretly bought the deeds to Mrs Flitcroft's house, and presented them to her.

But it took a long time for Ehrich the Great to become Houdini. As the King of Cards he worked at circuses, carnivals and indoor exhibitions. Sometimes he was booked to entertain at private parties, and it was at one of these that he met his wife. He performed a trick with a glass of coloured liquid, accidentally spilling it and ruining the dress of an attractive young lady,

Fig. 16. **Harry Houdini** (1874–1926), the greatest escape artist of all time. *Photo from the Davenport Collection.*

Miss Bessie Rahner. Too poor to pay for the damage, Harry got his mother to make a new dress for the girl, who soon afterwards became his wife.

They travelled all over the vastness of America, earning very little, and with the knowledge that their marriage was disapproved of by both his parents and hers. The brave young couple were of different religions. In their newly formed double-act, 'The Houdinis: Harry and Bessie', they astonishingly changed places. He locked her inside a trunk, and was himself restrained in a sack. After only a few seconds, Bessie would be found to be sealed in the sack, and Harry would emerge from the trunk.

Entitled 'Metamorphosis', it was the climax to an act in which they presented much small magic. But it was not until he dropped the card-tricks and other feats of presto-changeo that Harry started to make good. 'Give 'em a hint of danger, even of death,' was the advice given to him by a publicity man in 1895. Harry took the advice to heart, and within a few short years he had risen from an obscure circus act to an international headliner in the world's greatest variety houses.

Since his death in 1926 there have been at least twenty books written about Houdini, two films and countless magazine articles. I have read them all in some attempt to get an idea of what he was really like as a performer. Until a short while ago I discovered nothing that would explain what it was that made him able to make such a success with a form of entertainment considered by many to be old-fashioned, even at the turn of the century. At last I discovered the answer, by way of a scratchy tape-recording of a talk given by the famous magician Dunninger. The speaker, in his eighties at the time of the recording, had complete recall concerning Houdini's performance. He described him thus:

'Imagine the scene, as this homely-looking man, below average height and slightly bow-legged, walked out onto the vastness of the stage of the New York Hippodrome. One hand behind him, like Napoleon in reverse, he placed a foot on the footlights, leaned forward and treated his audience to the most wonderful smile in showbusiness.'

So there it was: the answer, or part of it. Houdini was not a big success just because he could escape from restraints; he was obviously magnetic, a very great showman. One can imagine what followed, as Houdini made his opening address to the audience:

'Ladies and gentlemen, I am Houdini. I defy any public body or private citizen to restrain me, in such a manner that I cannot escape. I accept all challenges and dares. No power on earth can hold Houdini!'

There is no recording of Houdini's voice, but I understand that he spoke with a strong New York accent, of the kind associated with the Bronx. Obviously he could project his voice and his personality to the furthest seat in the largest theatre.

Wherever he appeared the public took him at his word, and devised new restraints to test him with. One night it would be a safe, another it would be a new-style handcuff, and packing-case makers would vie with each other for the publicity that a challenge to Houdini would bring.

Houdini had a small curtained cabinet on the stage, into which he could be placed in order to effect his escapes in privacy. Sometimes he would emerge, through the curtains, smiling and free, in a matter of a few minutes. At other times he would not appear until the audience were convinced that the great Houdini had failed, at last. These intervals did not depend upon the difficulty, or otherwise, that he encountered. If he escaped quickly he would sit and read a dime novel, with the aid of an electric torch, until he considered that the time was right to emerge! Such was the strength of his personality that his audiences would wait patiently, however long it took.

In addition to his stage performances, Houdini would present outdoor stunts in all the cities where he appeared. In localities with good local sea or river conditions, he would show his famous underwater escape. Handcuffed and locked into a sack, he would be placed into a packing-case, its lid firmly nailed by local carpenters. Then, usually in front of the largest crowd ever to assemble in that place, he would allow the packing-case, suitably weighted, to be dropped into the water. Minutes later, when everyone was convinced that he had drowned, he would break the surface of the water, waving the handcuffs. Of course the newspaper publicity that this free show produced would make certain of full houses for Houdini at the theatre for the whole week.

On 27 November 1906 Houdini prepared to perform his underwater escape from the Belle Island Bridge, Detroit. The extra cold spell had caused the river to freeze over, but too many people had gathered to watch him for Houdini to call off his stunt. He had a hole sawn in the ice, and gave instructions for the weighted packing case to be dropped through the hole. When, after five minutes, he had not reappeared, everyone present suspected that he had perished. At the end of ten minutes they were convinced of it. Well, Houdini did reappear, but not in time to prevent an extra edition of the local paper going to press with the news of his death!

Houdini had of course escaped in his usual manner, and made upwards with every intention of emerging through the hole in the ice. But in that murky water he was unable to locate it. Although he could, through training, hold his breath longer than most swimmers, he was in trouble after a couple of minutes. Fortunately he did not panic, but remembered that there is a life-saving oxygen layer just below the surface of the ice. He floated up again and again, filling his lungs, before each fresh search for the hole.

Bessie was slightly unwell with flu that day, and was confined to their hotel room. She heard the newsboys calling: 'Houdini dead!' and all but fainted from shock and relief when the dripping wet Harry walked into the room.

Of course Houdini got enormous publicity from this escape. He was his own best publicity-man, which is why people are still talking about him.

Offstage, Houdini was endowed with many good qualities, and his kind and charitable acts were well known. But there was another side to his character. He was ruthless in his dealings with professional rivals, or people who crossed him in any way. He had a sharp temper, even if his outbursts were of short duration. The famous London magical dealer, Will Goldston, once told the story of what happened when Houdini visited him at his home in Hampstead. The American saw a painting on the wall which, he assured Goldston, had been promised to him by the artist. Goldston, who had bought the painting in good faith, said, 'Harry, your friendship means more to me than a paint-

March 21, 1921.

Houdini

My dear Will Goldston:

Many thanks for the Magazine of Magic which has just come.

Please be assured that I regret exceedingly not to be able to be with you this year at the big Savoy Dinner. My best wishes to Arthur Prince, whom I admire both as an artist and a gentleman.

Good Luck to the Club.

With every good wish for the success of your dinner,

Sincerely and fraternally yours,

Houdini

Fig. 17. A hitherto unpublished letter from Houdini to Will Goldston dated 21 March 1921. *From the Houdini files in the Davenport Collection.*

ing!' Houdini nodded, removed the painting from the wall, and took it with him when he left.

Since his death on Hallowe'en in 1926, Houdini has become a legend. Everything he did has become exaggerated, not least the manner of his death. His demise has been connected by many writers to his famous 'Chinese Water Torture Cell'. In this escape he was lowered, head first, into a glass tank full of water, his ankles secured in stocks. A curtain was lowered, and to increase the excitement, two firemen armed with axes stood by, ready to break the glass after a three-minute interval. Harry would never reappear until the audience were screaming at the firemen to break the glass!

But the actual cause of his death was somewhat less sensational. He was playing in Montreal, Canada, when some students from McGill University called backstage. One of them enquired if it were true that Houdini could withstand heavy blows to the stomach. Harry's mind was elsewhere and he nodded. One student took this to mean that he might strike a blow at Houdini's abdomen, which is what he did. Although shocked and hurt, the escape artist made light of the incident. Two days later, while playing Detroit, he was rushed to hospital in great agony, where an operation for peritonitis failed to save his life. He died in Bessie's arms.

Following the death of his mother, whom he had adored, in 1912, Houdini had become greatly interested in spiritualism. However, after many years of trying to contact his mother through a series of mediums, he suddenly decided, and publically announced, that all spirit mediums were frauds. Sir Arthur Conan-Doyle, creator of Sherlock Holmes, became Harry's friend and tried to convince him of the possibility of contacting the spirit world. Houdini maintained that it was strange for the inventor of such a famous detective to be so easily fooled. Indeed, Houdini's last few years as a performer were characterised by the inclusion at every show of exposés of the methods of fake mediums. But it is obvious that some lingering doubt on the subject remained in his mind, for he told Bessie that if it were possible to contact her from the spirit world he would do so. Alas, poor Bessie held seances on Hallowe'en and on Harry's birthday for twenty years, without any success.

'Excelsior London *Times* says greater than Houdini six months contract at eighty per week love Murray.'

This was the cablegram sent to Mrs Carrington-Walters in Australia by her son Norman in London on 26 February 1926. Norman Carrington-Walters had left his Melbourne home some ten years before, to gain fame as a magician and escape-artist. Like Houdini before him, he had needed to change his name and his style of work in order to gain success. He called himself Murray after Australia's most famous river.

Up to the time when he was able to send his mother such good news, he had worked his way to America as a ship's boy, played in vaudeville as a magician and barnstormed his way through eighty different countries. As with Houdini, he had to sacrifice much of his beloved magic and concentrate on dangerous escapes to gain fame. Indeed, when he returned to Australia in 1923 he had not completely learned the lesson. It was at a performance in an outdoor arena in Darwin that the turning point came.

After the usual card-tricks and bunny-vanishes had been coolly received, Murray invited one or two 'sportsmen' onto the stage to supervise his restraints. Two burly sailors chained and padlocked him, not exactly as directed. They placed him in his canvas cabinet, and one of them, not too sober, jogged the kerosene lamp which served as stage lighting. It was a gusty night, and the flames soon licked along the trail of kerosene, and shortly the canvas cabinet was ablaze. Murray, helpless to fight the fire in his chains, escaped in record time to emerge from the burning cabinet to a storm of applause. He had learned the same lesson as Houdini: 'Give 'em a hint of danger, even of death!'

Encouraged by the audience reaction, Murray changed his

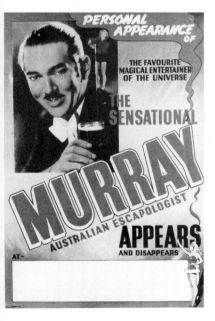

Fig. 18. Poster for **Murray**, the brilliant Australian showman, illusionist and escape artist, who coined the term 'escapologist'. *From the Davenport Collection.*

act so that every escape had a hint of real danger. He wanted a word to describe what he did on the posters, so he invented the word 'escapologist'.

When Murray arrived in London in 1926 he was still living in the shadow of the then more famous Houdini. But when an audition convinced the executives of the Stoll Theatre group to give him a trial week at the Empire Theatre, Ardwick, a suburb of Manchester. Murray was a big-enough success to secure a booking at the London Coliseum, at that time one of the most famous variety theatres in the world.

Like Houdini, Murray featured outside stunts to gain publicity. In one of these he conspired with the Fox Film Company to make use of their huge hoarding in Piccadilly Circus, the idea being that Murray should be restrained in a strait-jacket, and hung upside-down 150 feet above the traffic. But the important thing was that the newsreel cameras and press photographers would produce pictures clearly showing the hoarding. For thirteen and a half minutes Murray struggled, high above Eros, with the strait-jacket that he was beginning to think he was well qualified to wear! The escape effected, he beat a hasty retreat to avoid being arrested for stopping the traffic. The films being advertised on the hoarding were *One Slip* and *What Price Glory*!

In Cape Town, South Africa, Murray performed his packing-case escape for George Bernard Shaw. When a reporter asked G.B.S. for a comment, he said: 'I find the man even more interesting than the trick!'

While in Cape Town Murray met a stuntman who was performing delayed parachute-jumps. He suggested that Murray should try it, and the Australian said he would, but with his hands tied behind him. This meant that Murray would have to free his hands in record time in order to be able to pull the ripcord. He had never made a jump before and, in his innocence, imagined that he would fall feet first all the way down. When he had seen the stuntman turning over and over he had assumed that this was deliberate showmanship! Murray says: 'It seemed like an hour before I got my hands free and pulled the cord . . . and another hour before that heavenly white cloud billowed out over me!'

In 1933, during the winter season of Bertram Mills' Circus, at London's Olympia, Murray donned the strait-jacket again.

Thus restrained he was thrown into the big cage with seven performing lions. As the silence was broken only by the click-click of the newsreel cameras, and seven tawny shapes started to streak toward him, he said to himself, 'Murray, I think you've made a mistake. . .'

The fact that Murray survives still, at the age of eighty-two, to operate his Blackpool magic shop, tells you that he did indeed escape.

There have been other famous escapologists: for example, Val Walker, who appeared in naval officers' dress and called himself the Wizard of the Navy. Theo Hardeen worked very much in the style of Houdini. This was hardly surprising, as Houdini and Hardeen were brothers, a fact not widely known outside the profession. The two used to stage rivalries and feuds. This was a shrewd idea, with Hardeen playing the best of the theatres that were not important enough for Houdini to play, which kept genuine rivals away. After Houdini's death, Hardeen continued in the entertainment business, appearing with Olsen and Johnson in *Hellzapoppin'* in 1945.

One would imagine that Houdini, Murray and the other greats in the field had exhausted all the possibilities for escape effects. Yet in 1948 a young man burst into the field to introduce for the first time a fresh angle, perhaps the most dangerous of all. Alan Alan invented the now widely used 'Burning Rope'. The theme was that the escapologist was restrained with many feet of chain, and suspended upside-down at a height of perhaps sixty feet. Enough for anyone? But Alan had the rope from which he was suspended examined, and then soaked in paraffin and set alight. Alan had to escape and descend before the flames consumed the rope. In 1973, under canvas at Clapham Common with the Enis Togni Circus, Alan added yet another element. He performed the escape, as already described, over the open top of a cage full of wild-bred lions. Although he has not yet finally retired from being an escape-artist, Alan spends a lot of his time behind the counter of his magic shop.

The 'Chinese Water Torture', the 'Burning Rope', these are dangerous enough. But I think that any professional escapologist would agree that the milk-churn escape is the most dangerous of all.

In this escape, the seemingly ordinary milk churn was given the closest scrutiny by people who were obviously not confederates of the performer. The lid of the churn was seen to bear steel straps, which fitted staples on the churn itself for padlocking purposes. By means of a chain of buckets the performer's assistants filled the churn with milk, until it was overflowing. The performer, in a bathing costume and aided by assistants, would jump feet first into the churn. This would naturally displace some of the milk, but enough remained to lap the very rim as the performer's head disappeared. The lid was padlocked, and a curtain dropped in front of the churn. After perhaps a minute, the performer would appear, dripping with milk, from behind the curtain. The churn was found to be still padlocked and full of milk. Without wishing to betray any professional secrets, I can assure you that a careless performer could easily drown in attempting this escape.

Houdini, Hardeen and Murray used milk supplied by local dairies who would compete to supply it free for the advertisement. During World War II Murray was forced to use water as milk was strictly rationed. It had less glamour than milk, but was equally dangerous.

I mentioned earlier that the escape act was thought to be old-fashioned, even as far back as 1900, until the Houdini revival. Yet even today there are a number of performers proving that there is still a big audience for this kind of work. Nick Jansen, Timothy Dill-Russell, Paul Mathews, Paul Denver, Eric Ward, Hans Moretti, Larry Barnes and the New Houdinis are a few names that come to mind. These new wave escape-artists have three people to thank for the continued popularity of this style of work: Houdini, who turned an old art into a million-dollar entertainment, Murray, who invented the word 'escapologist', and Alan Alan, who showed how a new dimension could always revive a seemingly exhausted medium.

It would seem hard at first thought to point a finger at that which makes escapology an entertainment. Are people seriously diverted by watching a man who has been restrained, free himself?

I think our all but inherited desire to see the underdog emerge, triumphant, has something to do with it. I believe that Houdini had a great advantage in being of small stature. This

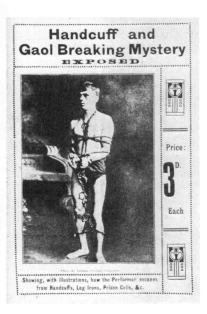

Fig. 19. An early twentieth-century booklet by W. Selby on escapology. *From the Davenport Collection.*

worked particularly to his advantage when he was tied or chained by large or burly people. One can imagine a large percentage of his audience being subconsciously outraged at the sight of two hulking bullies tying up the 'poor little fellow'. (The fact that the poor little fellow has boasted of his powers and demanded to be thus treated, is quite forgotten!)

Over the years, 'escape' novels have been a popular form of reading, and more recently a source of film material, from *The Count of Monte Cristo* and *The Man in the Iron Mask* to *The Wooden Horse.*

I would like to think that a desire to see innocence triumph over evil has a lot to do with it.

Three escape tricks

The Houdini handkerchief trick

The escapologist allows someone to tie his wrists together by means of passing a handkerchief around them and knotting it tightly. He then allows them to pass a length of rope between his arms, and to hold the two ends. After a few 'deft movements', the performer allows the spectator to pull on the rope, which appears to pass right through the handkerchief, which remains knotted around the performer's wrists.

Preparation: A pocket handkerchief and a length of soft rope, or string, about eight feet long.

Performance: During the showmanly 'gyrations', the performer gains some slack from the rope and passes it between his wrists by their movement. The fingers of one hand will complete the job, pulling the loop thus gained up to the fingertips. All that is necessary now is to insert the fingers of one hand through the loop. A sharp pull on the rope by the spectator will now free it, and make it appear to pass right through the handkerchief. Study the diagrams, which will make the operation of this simple trick even more clear.

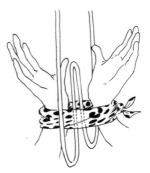

The escape ring

This is one of those little tricks which, once learned, can be presented in several different ways.

The performer's wrists are tied together by a piece of cord or string. The illustration shows that a length of cord spans between the wrists, due to the manner of the tie. This tying can be done by a member of the audience who can even be allowed to seal the knots with tape should he so wish. Next the performer picks up and shows a bangle, which can be minutely examined. The performer turns his back to the audience for only a few seconds. When he turns to face them again, the bangle is threaded on the cord which spans the wrists. The knots are intact.

Preparation: You will need a length of soft cord or string, about two feet long, two identical bangles which are large enough to be worn, not only on the wrists, but further up the arm. The performer needs to wear a jacket. Before the performance, push one bangle over one hand, and slide it up about half-way to the elbow. This is not seen due to the jacket being worn.

Performance: Have the wrists tied as illustrated, and pick up and show the second bangle. This is the only one of which the audience are aware. Turn your back and swiftly drop the second bangle into an inside jacket pocket, while sliding the first bangle down the arm, over the hand and onto the string or cord.

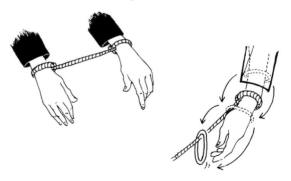

If you wish, you can start out with one bangle inside the jacket. Have the wrists tied, as before, but with the other bangle openly threaded onto the string. When you turn your back, slide the bangle on the cord up your arm, and remove the other one from the coat. Turn and show that the bangle has 'escaped'!

37

Amazing escape ball

Here's a little trick which would have intrigued Houdini, as it features an escapologist in the shape of a solid wooden ball. The sphere has a hole drilled clean through it, and there is a small perspex box, into which the ball can comfortably be fitted. Two holes in the box can be lined up with that which passes through the ball.

Performance: Once the ball is in the box the magician passes two cords right through the box and ball, and ties them, so that the box and ball are made secure. Two spectators are invited to assist, each holding two ends of the cords. They are instructed to pull on the cords. As they do so, the ball falls out of the box and into the outstretched hand of the magician. An amazing escape indeed! This little trick, obtainable from your favourite magic shop (a stone's throw from Charing Cross), fits neatly into the pocket. You can tell your beholders some of the stories about Houdini that appear in this book. You can illustrate one of these by having the ball represent that great little escape-king.

Chapter 3
Chinese magic

If you were to ask the average person where he or she thought magic, as a performing art, originated, they would be likely to say 'China'. There are several reasons for this. To begin with the very appearance of a Chinese in traditional dress presents a picture of a magical being, rather like the wizard of mythology. Add to this the fact that China was closed to Europeans until about 150 years ago, so that it retained a reputation for a long time as a land of mystery.

Early explorers found Chinese conjurers performing in market-places, rather as they had found such performers in the already explored parts of the Orient. Accounts of their demonstrations would suggest that they specialised in the production of bowls and jars, filled with water or fruit. These brightly lacquered vessels were produced from beneath large shawls or squares of silk. Early etchings and drawings of such conjurers show that they also specialised in tricks with tissue-paper. In one such trick, the conjurer would tear up several squares of tissue and dip the resulting bundle into water. He would then wave a fan over the wet pieces, which would magically change to dry confetti.

In some cases we may well have mistaken drawings of jugglers for those of magicians. Fans, swords and metal rings used to juggle with could so easily be thought to be magician's properties. However, in 1830 a Chinese troupe appeared at Saville House in London, and featured in their repertoire the magical linking and unlinking of solid metal rings. The 'Chinese Rings', is perhaps to this day the best-known and most often performed magical routine in the world. But it is most often shown by magicians in European dress. In the classic form a number of the rings are counted and shown to be separate from each other. The rings are linked and unlinked,

39

seemingly at the will of the performer. People from the audience examine the linked rings and try to unlink them without success, but only the magician can do so at will.

Another interesting traditional Chinese trick is the 'Rice Bowls'. In this the conjurer shows two china or metal bowls, seemingly empty and innocent. One of the bowls is filled to its brim with rice, and the bowls are placed rim to rim. A little shake, and the bowls are parted to reveal that the rice has doubled in quantity. Then the rice is turned to water, and poured from bowl to bowl. Rice and the bowls from which it is usually eaten are items that would have been easily available in China, and most traditional Chinese tricks are with items that would have been readily to hand.

Not many genuine Chinese magicians have found favour in the West, but this does not mean that magic with a Chinese dressing has not been very popular. More often this has been presented by western magicians, disguised as Chinese, with suitable dress, properties and music.

But there was one notable exception, a genuine and very famous Chinese magician who called himself Ching Ling Foo. His real name was Che Ling-Qua, and he was born in Peking in 1854. He served a hard apprenticeship with a wandering juvenile troupe, but eventually became a solo magician in his own right, and a favourite with the Empress of China. He was in his forties, quite elderly for a Chinese in those days, before he was able to leave his native land and seek fame in America. There he created quite a sensation as a vaudeville act, performing magic which was distinctly novel to American audiences. He performed all the old Chinese productions of bowls from a cloth, but climaxed it all by the production of a living child. He produced ribbons, fire, and a large barber's pole from his mouth. It was in 1899, at Keith's Theatre in New York City, that Ching issued a challenge to other magicians. He offered a thousand dollars to any who could exactly duplicate his performance. The challenge was taken up by an American conjurer, William Ellsworth Robinson, who had toured extensively with Herrmann the Great, as an assistant, as well as on his own as Robinson, Man of Mystery. He was currently 'resting' and operating a bookstore when he heard about the challenge. He presented himself at the theatre in the full knowledge that he could duplicate Ching's tricks, and that he could use a thousand dollars! But Ching's manager told him that he could not exactly duplicate the performance, as in order to do so he would need to be Chinese. Robinson returned to his bookstore, realising that he had been 'had', and that the challenge had been just a publicity stunt.

But Robinson had his revenge by producing a Chinese act that was a very convincing imitation of that of Ching Ling Foo. He called himself 'Chung Ling Soo', and although he was not an immediate success in America, he brought the act to London in 1900, where at the Alhambra Theatre he scored a big hit. Offers to appear at theatres all over the British Isles soon poured in, and he was able to hire a genuine Chinese family to act as assistants. He added a number of big illusions to his act, one of which was with a giant Chinese lantern, which revolved, to produce several Chinese maidens, one after the other. From beneath a cone he produced a small tree, which would grow oranges, right before the eyes of the audience. These, Chung would pluck and distribute, to prove them genuine. Of course he was soon widely imitated, just as he had imitated Ching Ling Foo: but never equalled, possibly even to this day, for magic, colour and oriental spectacle.

For many years Robinson managed to keep his American nationality a secret, not only from the public but also from the press. He was careful never to be observed in public without his elaborate Chinese disguise. The tall Yankee, with the hard stetson hat, who was sometimes seen around the theatre, was thought by most to be his manager!

Sometimes Chung Ling Soo would hold a press conference, and would sit upon a throne, a fair distance from the reporters. One of the Chinese assistants would 'translate' the reporter's questions. He and Chung would confer, in a fake Chinese dialect, and then the assistant would give the answers in English. He would pretend to be Chung Ling Soo Junior, saying things like: 'My father, he tinkee Blitish people velly wonderful!'

Almost weekly, Robinson added new and exciting illusions to his act. He would fire a girl from a cannon, and she would arrive in a box, suspended in the roof of the theatre. Where other conjurers produced a three-foot long Union Jack, Robin-

Fig. 20. **Chung Ling Soo** (in reality a Scots American). *Photo from the Davenport Collection.*

son would produce one that covered the entire theatre back-cloth. Yet with all the spectacle of his show it was perhaps his masterly manipulation of the 'Chinese Rings' that made the biggest impact on the audience. In his hands the old Chinese trick became a big production. He used rings that were at least fourteen inches across, and very heavy, which made the trick more convincing. He would use twelve rings instead of the more usual eight, which meant that when he formed them into a great chain he required two assistants to help him spread them across the stage. Even if the trick had not been of Chinese origin, I believe that Chung Ling Soo's performance with them would have earned them the title of the 'Chinese Rings'.

By 1905 Robinson had established himself as the top illusion-ist in Britain. So it came as rather a shock when a rival appeared on the scene, in the shape of the original Ching Ling-Foo! The Chinese of course made much of the fact that Robinson had imitated his act, and objected to the similarity of name. But the public knew that Chung Ling Soo had the better show, so to them he had to be the genuine Chinese magician. Every night they filled the London Hippodrome, to see Chung Ling Soo,

Fig. 21. The magnificent gold-edged headed notepaper used by Chung Ling Soo, who lived on a grand scale. *From the Davenport Collection.*

and stayed away from the Empire, Leicester Square, where Ching Ling Foo was the headliner.

Ching decided that it was time to issue one of his famous challenges. He proposed a 'contest of magic' between himself and Robinson, that reporters might themselves decide who was the one and only great Chinese conjurer. A thousand-dollar stake was again proposed.

On the morning of 7 January 1905 a huge limosine arrived at the Fleet Street offices of the *Weekly Dispatch*. A crowd had gathered, of the kind that never misses a coronation or jubilee. They cheered as Chung Ling Soo and his retinue climbed out of the car, gasping at the sight of the magician's ermine-trimmed robes. This had to be the real Chinese conjurer, especially as Ching Ling Foo failed to put in an appearance.

Robinson put on the show that he had planned for the press, even if the contest was off. Later there was a press conference, with the use of the 'interpreter'. Ching Ling Foo and his thousand dollars had gone to France, the real Chinaman having seemingly lost interest in the whole affair. Naturally the papers claimed that Chung Ling Soo was the one and only genuine and marvellous Chinese conjurer!

Although he toured in India, Australia, and all over Europe, Robinson always returned to Great Britain, which became his adopted country. When World War I broke out, he had the opportunity to return to the safety of his native America, but preferred to stay in Britain and take his chance. He continued to tour during the war, despite great difficulties. He also did a great deal to raise money for war charities, and even amazed the soldiers at the Western Front, by appearing in the trenches in his full oriental disguise, to entertain them!

Periodically Robinson would present a 'grand added attraction' to his show in the form of the famous bullet-catching feat. In this he demonstrated his ability to catch, in his teeth, bullets fired at him from an antique gun. He was not of course the first magician to present this feat, which had a long and gruesome history. In 1631 Coullew of Lorraine died during its performance. In 1818 an Indian magician, Kia Khan Khruse, had died during a performance at the Pall Mall Theatre, Dublin, when a marksman had substituted his own bullet. At Arnstadt in 1820 a Polish conjurer's wife, Mme de Linsky, had been the target, and was fatally wounded. In 1826 the son of the French magician, Torrini, had died from a similar accident. Other victims had included Dr Epstein, in the ring of the Parisian Cirque d'Hiver in 1869, the son of de Line in New York in 1899, and Michael Hatel in the same city in 1906. Alexander Herrmann, who had for many years been Robinson's employer, had performed the feat just seven times, and warned his assistant to avoid it. But of course Robinson performed it, successfully, many times, until the fatal night of 23 March 1918.

It was a Saturday night, the last of his week's engagement at the Empire Theatre, Wood Green, in north London. In those days variety shows were so popular that two performances were given each night. It was near the end of the second performance that the tragedy occurred. The bullet trick had been widely advertised, so the theatre was comfortably filled. The audience had watched the two large muzzle-loading guns being loaded with bullets which they had themselves marked, and the usual

44

powder and wadding associated with such ancient weapons had been applied. There was a slow drum roll as Robinson raised the china dish, upon which he intended to drop the bullets from his mouth when he had caught them. He gave the signal and the marksman fired. The usual explosions and recoil from the guns, and for some seconds Chung Ling Soo stood like a statue. Then, to the astonishment of the audience, he fell heavily onto the stage. Following a bewildered silence there was a scattering of applause from some members of the audience who thought it was all part of the show. Then the curtain descended, the band played loudly and the puzzled audience dispersed. But behind that red plush curtain, William Ellsworth Robinson lay dying. Dot Path, his faithful assistant and companion of twenty-five years, cradled him in her arms. He died in the early hours of the following day. He was fifty-eight years old and had been a professional wonder-worker for forty years, almost half that time as Chung Ling Soo.

There was an inquest at the Wood Green coroner's court on 28 March 1918. The coroner took evidence from the doctor who

Fig. 22. One of the many superb posters of Chung Ling Soo. *From the Davenport Collection.*

had examined Robinson at the theatre, that death was from two gunshot wounds, both caused by the same bullet, on entering and emerging from his body. Scotland Yard's own gun expert, Robert Churchill, confirmed that a weakness in the mechanism of one of the trick guns involved had caused a bullet to discharge which should have stayed in the barrel. Death by misadventure was the verdict.

The seemingly ancient muzzle-loading guns were in fact made for the purpose, and were not genuine antiques. Each gun had a decorative tube below its single barrel. This appeared to hold a ramrod, but was in fact to hold a powder charge which would explode, harmlessly, when the weapon was fired. The bullet and powder, openly placed in the actual barrel, were not intended to leave the gun, as the butt end of the barrel was permanently sealed. However, Robinson had used the guns for many years, and a weakness or fault had developed in the metal seperating the real and trick barrel. A mere spark had been enough to fire the load which had never been intended to leave the gun.

Of course Chung Ling Soo was too famous for the publicity that attended the accident to die away quickly. Some journalists claimed that he had been murdered by a Chinese secret society, and illogically revealed at the same time that he was not really Chinese! Will Goldston, of the vivid imagination, claimed that his friend had committed suicide. He suggested that Robinson, tired of his impersonation, and worried by financial and domestic matters, had decided to doctor one of the guns, to bring about his own death. But it seems to us more than unlikely that a magician could go through with a two-hour show, knowing that he would die for its finale. It was in fact a sad and fatal accident.

Another Westerner to don oriental disguise to present a magical act was Theodore Bamberg, a Dutchman born in 1875, the fifth generation of a very famous magical family. He adopted the stage-name of Okito, first dressing himself and his act in Japanese style, but later, in the United States, where the Japanese were not all that popular, changing the act to a Chinese one. Okito was not an illusionist like Chung Ling Soo. He showed smaller feats of magic, many of his own invention, with great style and delicacy, and oriental colour. One of his most famous presentations was that of the 'Floating Ball'. In this a silver globe moved around mysteriously, floating in mid-air, even when a hoop was passed over it. The trick was not original to Okito, but his performance of it was so artistic that his name will always be remembered in connection with it. He constructed and beautifully decorated all of his own apparatus, and the pieces that he made are now prized as valuable collectors' items.

Okito's son, David Bamberg, born in 1904, also became a famous magician. Inspired by the character created by Sax Rohmer, he called himself Fu-Manchu. With so much competition in Europe and the United States, David wisely concentrated on South America, where he built a show of big illusions and became a considerable star. I think the biggest point of difference between Fu-Manchu and Chung Ling Soo was in the fact that although he wore robes and a little slanting line of make-up on each eye, David Bamberg made no attempt at a Chinese impersonation. It was as if, to him, the spirit of magic was in the Orient. This made it easier for him to present a varied programme, as he was not confined to Chinese settings and decor. Working in Mexico, Cuba and the other South American republics, he has also been a success in Spain and Portugal.

Another Spanish-speaking Chinaman was Juan Pablo, a Panamanian, who followed the illusionist's tradition by becoming Chinese. As Chang he presented a big, exotic illusion show throughout South America and was one of the few magicians to tour a magic circus under canvas.

During World War I a magician in Britain, Fang-Wu, who had been christened Joseph Banks, set up as a rival to Chung Ling Soo, although far less successful. When that great illusionist was so tragically killed at Wood Green, Banks was hired to present a show called *The Chung Ling Soo Mysteries*. But the public were well aware that it would not be the performer that they wanted to see, and the arrangement was soon discontinued. However, Joseph Banks' eldest son, Claude, took out a Chinese act during the 1920s under the name of Cingalee. This was a wonderful act, superbly dressed and rich in fine magic. The act ran until Cingalee died in 1965. The only criticism I ever heard of his act was that he 'worked too fast for a Chinese'!

It is difficult to find examples of genuine Chinese magicians who made good in Western show business. But one other than Ching Ling Foo managed to make a name in American vaudeville. He was Long Tack Sam, who first appeared in America at Hammerstein's Theatre, New York in 1915. He had his own company, the Pekinese Troupe, but before the New York booking had trouble obtaining engagements, as he was thought to be a dog act! He presented only four tricks, small ones, like the torn and restored paper strip. But when he died in 1961 he was a very wealthy man.

Although there have been so few real Chinese magicians on the theatre scene, the inspiration of Chinese magic will always be felt, the exotic scenes and decor being so suitable for magical presentation.

Chinese magic in miniature

Here are one or two tricks with a Chinese flavour that you might like to try. Do not despise the tricks for their simplicity, for many very effective tricks are based on simple principles. This is good, because it means that the magician, and that's you, can concentrate on presenting the tricks well.

The Chung-Ling-Soo coins

This is one of the tricks which Chung-Ling-Soo used to show to newspaper men at his famous press conferences. You can do it too, and may not even need to use an interpreter! It made use of half a dozen Chinese coins and a length of string, about eighteen inches long. The coins were of the old Chinese type with a hole through the centre but otherwise quite solid. If you cannot obtain suitable coins, you can do it with curtain-rings.

Soo would seemingly thread one of the coins on the string and secure it at the centre. Then he would double the string and pass the two ends through the holes in the other coins. He would give an end each to two of the reporters, so that the result looked like Diagram 1. He had made the tied coin support the others. Covering the coins and string with a handkerchief, he would plunge a hand under it and bring forth the five coins while the reporters still held the string. Then he would whisk away the handkerchief and show that the supporting ring was still in its place on the centre of the string.

Performance: In seeming to thread and secure the first coin, the dirty work is done. The loop of the doubled string was pushed through the hole (Diagram 2), then half of the coin was pushed through the loop and the string pulled tight (Diagram 3). The other coins were threaded on the string, so that when the ends were held, the threaded coin supported them all. Under cover of a handkerchief, Soo had only to reverse the moves with the supporting coin, releasing it, so that the other coins would drop free. Then, again under cover of the handkerchief he would replace the supporting coin, so that it looked undisturbed.

It is essential to retain the interest of the audience while going through these moves. Learn a little of the history of Chinese coinage, and give the people the benefit of your knowledge. Or do as Chung Ling Soo did, and gabble away in fake Chinese!

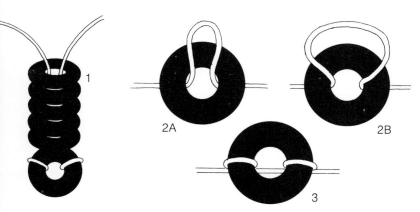

The Chinese compass

The magician shows an eight-sided disc which has an arrow on each side of it. When he pivots the disc, between the pads of his first finger and thumb, showing both sides, the arrows are seen to be both pointing in the same direction. However, when he alters the position of the arrow on one side, by a movement of the disc, and again turns it, the arrow on the other side, far from pointing in the same direction, now points to a different direction. The magician can adjust the position of the disc so that both arrows will again coincide.

Preparation: You can make the eight-sided disc from cardboard, or you can buy a smart little plastic model from your magic shop. Whichever, it should have an arrow on one side at right-angles to the arrow on the other side.

Experiment with it, and you will soon amaze yourself! There are, you will find, only two positions at which the compass can be revolved to gain no change in the arrow, if it is adjusted to roughly north-east or south-west. The change in the direction of the arrow when the disc is adjusted so that the arrow points any other way is startling!

Performance: This little gadget can be very amusing to use, as if it were a compass, particularly if you are fooling your

RIGHT HAND
FINGERS PUSH
× PIVOT THE
COMPASS

DOTTED LINE
INDICATES ARROW
ON REVERSE SIDE

friends that you are trying to find your way
somewhere by its aid!

Spot the spots

Here is a pocket trick with two little paddles, held
between the conjurer's thumb and forefinger, as in
the diagrams below. By turning his hand over, the
conjurer demonstrates that each of the two paddles
has a spot on each side. Yet with a quick movement of
the hand, all the spots can be made to appear on one of
the paddles, two on each side. The other paddle
appears to be perfectly blank on both sides. The spots
can be made, by means of another flick of the wrist, to
regain their original positions. During certain stages
of the trick the paddles can be examined. They come
to you complete with full instructions, under the
above title, from your friendly Charing Cross magic
shop.

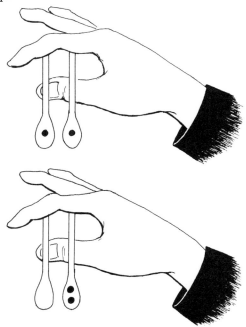

Chapter 4
Fire and water

The dangerous element of fire has been both worshipped and feared by mankind. Worshipped as the great source of heat and light, the means by which food could be cooked, and the only sure way to keep wild beasts at bay; feared as that great force of destruction, seeming at times to appear as if by magic. Early mountebanks and showmen learned to play with fire, some even to eat it, while others juggled with sticks that had been set ablaze. Witch-doctors learned to make much of fire, and Indian fakirs walked barefooted on the smouldering hot ashes of a fire.

Magicians of the entertainment variety have not used fire extensively, the best-known trick with it being the production of a blazing metal bowl from beneath a cloth. Its sudden production has been a favourite opening trick with magicians for two centuries. A trick of early Chinese origin involves the placing of smouldering tow into the mouth and the blowing forth of sparks and even flames. All of these things are best avoided by the aspiring wizard!

On a larger scale, the 'Cremation Illusion' was a bizarre mystery. In it a girl was laid in a coffin, a cloth or piece of sacking placed over her and ignited. After a sheet of flame had arisen, the sides of the coffin would drop, to reveal only a ghastly heap of ashes. Usually the lady would make a reappearance from elsewhere, for example running down the centre aisle of the theatre, shouting, 'Here I am . . . I'm all right!' There is a legend you might hear told and retold in magical circles, of a very famous presentation of this illusion. The magician who presented it was playing at a variety theatre which was very close to a playhouse. The girl involved had to leave the variety theatre by the stage door, circle the building and re-enter through the main doors in order to gain the centre aisle. On the first night she circled the building, took a wrong turn, and by accident entered the main doors of the playhouse. The magician waited in vain for his lady to reappear. But the audience at the playhouse were treated to the spectacle of a girl in spangles, unaccountably running down the centre aisle and shouting 'Here I am!' in the middle of Hamlet's soliloquy!

One famous illusionist perished in a theatre fire, and his death presented a mystery more bizarre than any that he presented on the stage. He was Sigmund Neuberger, famous as the Great Lafayette.

Following the turn of the century Lafayette created a spectacular show of illusions and quick changes. As a Chinaman, he would paint a large lightning portrait of a musical director. He would then exit and immediately re-enter by bursting through the portrait, in evening dress and carrying a baton. In another scene a quite obviously live lion would roar and pace in its cage. A girl in a bridal gown was thrust into the cage. But the lion, far from attacking her, would rear up and remove its skin to reveal itself as the Great Lafayette! A thrilling quick change, as well as a magical illusion involving a real lion. Later in the show he enacted a magical playlet, riding a white horse.

Lafayette was a somewhat eccentric man, to say the least. He drilled his assistants like soldiers, and insisted that they salute him in the street. He enjoyed a lavish lifestyle, yet seemed entirely without human companionship. He lavished all his affection on a small cross-bred terrier called Beauty. The little dog had been given to him by Harry Houdini, who could not have suspected that the little animal was destined to sleep on velvet cushions, and dine at table with its master. Beauty wore a collar studded with real diamonds, and over the entrance to Lafayette's London home was a plaque: 'The more I see of men the more I love my dog'. Her likeness decorated the illusionist's cheques, headed note-paper and contract forms. A gold statuette of Beauty replaced the usual figure on the bonnet of her master's Rolls-Royce.

So lavish did Lafayette's show become that he was forced to play for two weeks in each town, rather than the more usual one-week engagement. He opened one such two-week season in Edinburgh, Scotland, on 1 May 1911. But the engagement, which opened with a great flourish, was soon to become a time of tragedy for Lafayette. On 5 May Beauty died at the age of thirteen, probably as a result of over-nourishment. Lafayette was refused permission to bury her in an £800 vault at Pierhill cemetery, but solved the problem by stating that the vault was to be his own last resting place.

On 9 May a fire broke out on the stage, a lit brazier, part of the oriental decor, catching a flimsy drapery. Although the asbestos safety curtain (fitted in all theatres at that time for just such an emergency) was lowered, there was by all accounts quite a panic among the audience, with more than two thousand people trying to get out of the theatre as quickly as they could. But that was nothing to the panic that developed backstage. As the fire took a hold there was a blazing inferno, with many casualties and ten people burnt to death. The lion survived, though singed, and the charred body of Lafayette was found near the cage. His body could be identified only from his costume and the sword that he carried. The body was cremated, and the ashes placed between the paws of Lafayette's only friend in the vault.

But even in death, Lafayette was to enact another mystery, a transposition more bizarre than any he had presented on the stage. . . .

Some eye-witnesses suddenly announced that they had seen Lafayette leave, and then re-enter the theatre, to save his white horse, it was thought. Then a lawyer, who had transacted business for the illusionist, enquired about Lafayette's diamond rings, which he knew him to wear at all times. These had not been found on the body, and a further search of the theatre revealed another charred body, dressed exactly as Lafayette had been, and wearing the missing diamonds! Lafayette had used doubles in some of his illusions in order to appear in two places at once. This second body was obviously that of Lafayette.

The inquest which followed revealed that the fire had been started not from the brazier but by a fault in an electrical contraption attached to the metal floor of the lion's cage. Lions are languid creatures and Lafayette made sure that it would be lively by giving it mild electric shocks. It is strange that a man who loved his dog so much could be so cruel to a lion.

But this evidence was not in time to prevent the cremation, and placing of the wrong ashes in the vault. The great magicians of the world sent floral tributes, that from Houdini being a floral replica of the friend that he had given to Lafayette thirteen years before.

Water is another element that has been rejoiced at, through its life-giving qualities, from the earliest times. It has been used in magic rather more than has fire. Chinese conjurers turned rice into water, and Indian magicians produced a seemingly never-ending stream of water from a half coconut shell. Western conjurers turned water to wine and vice versa. Great illusionists like Kalanag and Levante poured all the world's beverages from a jug of clear water. This liquid producing, a continuation of the inexhaustible bottle of Robert-Houdin, naturally depends on water in all its variations, and has always been very popular with audiences. Also newspaper critics trying to think of something to say about the magic show, which they may not always be qualified to judge, will grab at the chance to use the liquid-producing trick as a talking point. 'What a great fellow to invite to a party . . . you could never run out of drinks!' The great English conjurer of the early 1900s, David Devant, poured any drink called for by his audience from a tea-kettle. The invention of the 'Magic Kettle' was not Devant's, but that of a then very young conjurer, Chris Charlton. Many years later, when he was an elderly man, Chris told me how this had come about. It seems that as a schoolboy conjurer he was featuring two tricks: the 'Inexhaustible Bottle' and a tea-kettle that boiled when placed upon a block of ice. Suddenly he thought how very effective it would be if he were able to pour the drinks from the kettle. So he made a new version of the drinks trick, building the works from the bottle into a kettle. He sold the result to David Devant, who had it remade and improved by his mechanic, Henry Bate. Devant soon knew that he had a hit on his hands, when he first presented it at Maskelyne's theatre.

Perhaps the most famous trick with water was that of the 'Chinese Water Fountains' featured by magicians like Dante and Howard Thurston. The illusionist produces thin streams of water from the heads, fingers and elbows of a stageful of assistants, usually in oriental garb. With the correct lighting and music it can be a spectacular and pleasing effect.

Other effective tricks with water include the 'Hydrostatic

Glass' in which water stays put in an inverted tumbler, until the magician permits it to spill. And the 'Magic Funnel', generally used in comedy effects to tap excess liquid from the elbow of an assistant.

Water, in the form of a great ocean, played a dramatic part in the life of Horace Goldin, one of the brightest stars in magic's history.

Goldin was born Hyman Goldstein in a ghetto at Vilna in Russian-occupied Poland, in 1873. His family emigrated to America, to escape persecution, when he was sixteen. He worked as a shop assistant in Nashville, Tennessee, until becoming the apprentice of a touring showman, Adolph Veidt. It was Veidt, an Austrian, who gave him his stage name and set him on the path to magical fame. Goldin stammered, and spoke little English, so he adopted a silent act, working fast, to lively music. He showed great originality, and in the years that followed would invent a full hundred tricks and illusions, including 'Walking Through a Sheet of Glass', 'Sawing a Woman in Half', 'Film to Life' and the 'Canary in the Light-Bulb'. In 1901 he arrived in London to appear at the Palace Theatre, where his originality and whirlwind style created a sensation. So much so that in November 1902 he was invited to entertain King Edward VII and Queen Alexandra at Sandringham, with the King's cousin, the Kaiser, also being present.

Goldin had an artist prepare huge replicas of the tiny diamond and ruby pins given to him by the Kaiser and the King. He billed himself from that time as the 'Royal Illusionist'. In 1913 he undertook a world tour, during which he entertained the King of Siam and his wives in a theatre that the monarch had had built specially for the occasion.

Like many otherwise shrewd men, Goldin had a blind-spot: and he distrusted banks and insurance companies. This meant that he not only had not insured the properties of his show, but that he transported his life-savings, in gold-bars, everywhere he went, in a metal box!

At Lahaina, Hawaii, in July 1918, the illusionist was standing on the deck of an ocean liner, watching the small boats filled with his equipment and animals being brought from the quay to the ship, when a sudden storm, of a kind not uncommon off

56

Fig 23. A rare poster of **Horace Goldin**, the Royal Illusionist, who performed at a whirlwind pace and revolutionised the speed of magic during the early 1920's. *From the Davenport Collection.*

Hawaii, sank all the boats. None of his equipment or his cash-box was recovered, and worse for the sentimental Goldin, his beautiful Bengal tigress, Ranee, was drowned in her travelling crate. She was his pet as well as being a valuable member of his company.

But there was one property that had not descended to the depths, because it was in Goldin's pocket. A small black bag, containing an egg. His egg-bag was the effect that had most intrigued Edward VII. With the change in his pocket, Goldin purchased two packs of cards. With these and his egg-bag, he was able to present an act and earn money. He returned to the kind of engagements that he had been occupied with before he had become famous, and soon had earned enough to start to build a new show. But his real short-cut back to fame and fortune came in 1921. For it was in that year that he invented and built the illusion which was destined to become the most famous ever, 'Sawing a Woman in Half'.

A hushed audience at New York's Palace Theatre watched an attractive girl placed in an oblong box, with four doors showing the simplicity of its construction. Her neck was fixed in stocks, as were her hands, at one end, and her ankles secured in like fashion at the other. So her head, hands and feet were clearly seen, even when the four doors of the box were closed. Women fainted as the box was sawn right through. The audience gasped, as they saw the two halves of the box drawn apart, with the moving hands and head still projecting from one half, and the lively feet from the other! Goldin explained in his halting English that what he had done, anyone could do, and go to prison. But, he suggested, only a magician could put the poor girl together again. This he did, nudging the two halves of the box together, and opening the doors to reveal the girl quite whole.

Goldin could probably have papered the walls of his apartment with the press notices and write-ups that the illusion produced. He received so many offers to present the illusion in towns and cities all over America that he was forced to hire five other illusionists to take 'Sawing a Woman in Half' on tour. It is estimated that Goldin earned a million dollars from the one illusion, and lost most of it in courts of law, trying to protect his invention from imitators. However, when he arrived again in Britain in 1928, the illusionist was again at the head of his own big company and presenting a show to rival the one lost at sea. Those who said that he had not changed were wrong, for he now trusted banks and insurance companies.

In his later years Goldin became a British citizen, declaring that he wanted to throw in his lot with the people who had twice made him a star. In 1935 Dante arrived, presenting 'Sawing a Woman in Half' and claiming its invention, but when he saw Goldin's new version, with a power-saw and no covering box, he took it out of his show!

Curiously, Goldin died shortly after presenting the bullet-catching trick on the very stage where Chung Ling Soo had perished. But Goldin died of a heart attack, in the early hours of Tuesday, 22 August 1939, at the age of sixty-six. The immigrant boy, plump, not good-looking, with a stammer and little English, had been an entertainer of kings, inventor of a hundred great illusions, made and lost half a dozen fortunes and been a citizen of three countries.

Levitations with liquid are very effective because everyone knows the sort of disaster that can occur if the trick goes wrong! Here are two little tricks which are impressive. The first is of a seemingly impromptu nature, the second rather more 'stagey'.

Pop-bottle-puzzle

The effect is that the conjurer shows a plain glass bottle of the type used for minerals. It contains clear water. Our hero places his fingers over the neck of the bottle and then turns it upside down. There is no stopper in the bottle, yet he removes his fingers, and the water does not drop out. Of course there may be terribly suspicious people in the audience who think you may have deposited a stopper in the bottle when you placed your fingers over the opening. But all their suspicions are dispersed when the conjurer takes a match, inserts it in the opening, and allows it to float up, into the liquid! The conjurer dries the bottle with a handkerchief, prior to pouring out the liquid.

Preparation: You will need a little gadget which you can buy for a very small sum from your magic shop. The diagram will show you that it is a disc, with a rim, which will fit over most bottle tops. It is transparent, and it has a small hole in its centre. They are usually sold in packets of two or more.

Have the disc in a handy pocket and a handkerchief in another. A suitable bottle with clear water in it should be handy.

Performance: Pour out some of the liquid into a glass, at the same time getting the disc into one of your hands, from the pocket. Hold the bottle the right way up, and place the fingers over it, putting the disc in place, and leaving the fingers there as the bottle is turned upside-

59

down. Gently withdraw the fingers and you will find
that the disc stays put and no more than a drop of
water is spilled. The match can be inserted and will
float up to the surface of the water. In fact several
matches can be treated in this way, and if any member
of the audience has a knitting needle, that can be
gently inserted through the hole and as gently with-
drawn. The disc, being transparent, will not be seen.
Turning the bottle the right way up and mopping it
with the handkerchief is a good way of disposing of
the disc gadget.

You can use other liquids instead of water, but be
careful with aerated drinks that the bottle has been
uncorked for a while, otherwise it might fizz, foam or
otherwise cause problems!

TRANSPARENT
'STOPPER'
WITH HOLE

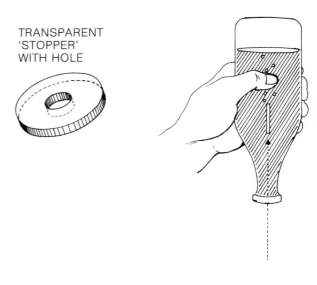

Water levitation

In this splendid little trick, a straight-sided metal
bowl is shown, shallow, circular, looking rather like
something made to hold paper-clips in an office. The
magician fills it almost to the brim with practically any

sort of liquid. He then places a playing-card or other cardboard square over it and turns the vessel upside down. He removes the card, and the liquid does not spill! He replaces the card, turns the vessel over, takes the card away and pours liquid from the bowl.

Preparation: The bowl, available at most magic shops, has a loose circular disc, lying on its bottom, and a lip around the rim. It should be all but overfilled with liquid.

Performance: When the card is placed over the mouth, the bowl inverted and nothing spilled the audience will not be impressed, having seen the old scientific experiment, but they will gasp when you take the card away. How can you do it?

Well, when you turn the bowl over, you will have to support the card for a second or two with a fingertip, and count mentally to ten before taking it away. That's about how long the metal disc takes to travel down and drop in place, just inside the top of the bowl. This will prevent the water falling, and if you reverse all your moves you can bring this trick to an impressive conclusion.

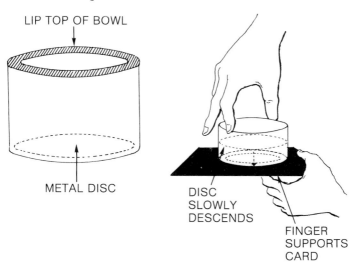

LIP TOP OF BOWL

METAL DISC

DISC SLOWLY DESCENDS

FINGER SUPPORTS CARD

61

Inflammable sugar

A sugar lump is not the easiest thing to set alight, but that is just what the conjurer is able to do. How? Well, shortly before he presents the effect, he quietly takes a sugar-lump from the bowl, and dips it in cigar-ash in the ashtray. When lit a splendid little blue flame will result.

Upon my sole!

A safety match can normally only be struck on the side of its box. But the magician is able to strike one on the sole of his shoe. He is able to do so because he has had the foresight to break one of the striking edges from a matchbox, and glue it to the sole of his shoe, onto that portion between sole and heel which never touches the ground.

The relit match

The party entertainer takes a match from an ashtray, a quite obviously used and burnt match, and strikes it to produce a flame!

The match is in fact an unused one, which has been pared down with a penknife, just below its head, and dipped into Indian ink. This gives a perfect burnt-match illusion. If you don't want the bother of making such matches you can buy boxes of them at magic and joke shops.

MATCH, SHAVED DOWN
BELOW HEAD,
DIPPED IN INDIAN
INK AND DRIED

If you plant one or two of these matches in an ashtray, you will be able to amaze everyone. But you may have difficulty in telling the trick matches from the really burned ones!

Chapter 5
The quickness of the hand

It is interesting the way people get hold of a phrase to explain away the feats of a magician, such as 'Simple, when you know how'. Most good tricks are not the result of one simple secret, but a great deal of hard work in invention, and a lot of practice before it can be performed. Another popular phrase is, 'The quickness of the hand deceives the eye.' What the onlooker puts to 'quickness' is in fact deftness, for speed will have little to do with it.

Let us consider the old racecourse swindle 'Find the Lady'. Whenever a shyster sets up in business with three cards on top of a packing-case on a street corner, there are always people who think that their sharp vision and quick reflexes will enable them to win. The operator, who shows you two aces and a queen, lays them face down and invites you to 'Find the Lady', may do so with swift movements. But that which he does, in order to ensure that you do not find the queen, will be slow, sure and calculated. If for example he should substitute another card for the queen, which he will surely do at some point, then he will certainly not chance his arm with some wild, furtive movement. The dirty work will have been done long before the card is turned over.

The three-card man has made quite a comeback in recent years, especially in big cities and tourist resorts. In its original form, the 'Three Card Monte', to give it the proper name, was a legitimate gambling game. The operator showed the faces of the cards, threw them on the table, moved them around, and the people made bets on which card was the queen. This genuine game of chance only became a swindle if the operator substituted or 'switched in' another card for the queen. After all, if no queen existed, the punter could not possibly find it! Unlike the magician, the three-card man performs only one trick, so he can perfect it to a really astounding degree and learn every 'twist' possible with it.

His first problem is to get a suspicious public to bet on the cards. He gets round this by using confederates, usually referred to in his circle as 'ricks'. The routine is that the 'rick' makes a bet, wins and is paid. This may be repeated several times, and some three-card men even allow a genuine member of the public to win at this stage. Then the stakes are raised, and the public lose their money. Most will wisely go home, but others, gripped by a gambling fever, will stay to try and recoup their losses. Sometimes the operator will deliberately bend the corner of the queen, as if by accident. The rick will point this out to a punter, in the hope that he will greatly increase his stake. But the cunning three-card man will have straightened the bend and substituted another bent card for one of the others, by the time the punter points to it. Of course the three-card man must be very adept at the few sleight of hand moves that he uses. But he must be even more skilled as an actor. Often more than one rick is employed, and, indeed, I have observed an occasion when the crowd consisted of four ricks and one punter! The gang needs only one wealthy loser to make the whole operation worthwhile. Often the ricks will be roughly dressed, in imitation of the type of people that would usually hang around a particular area, but they can sometimes be spotted by their expensive shoes, which they seldom bother to change.

What if the three-card man makes a mistake, and I win, you may ask. Do not delude yourself: these are hard, ruthless people who will even resort to violence as a last resource. Had you observed them, as I have, in a cafe following a session, dividing their spoils, you would not need advice to avoid them!

Another street swindle, also to be seen at racecourses, is the 'Shell Game'. It involves three half walnut shells and a pea. The pea is covered with one of the shells and the three shells are moved around. The punter bets on which shell he thinks the pea is under. Here he has less chance of winning than he has of finding the 'Lady' in the three-card trick. For this swindle is based on an Indian version of the 'Cups and Balls' in which very shallow cups were used.

Sometimes friends have said to me: 'How terrible it would be if you were to become dishonest and turn your knowledge of magic and sleight of hand toward fleecing the public!' Their imaginations run away with them. The mind of a conjurer is quite different from that of a confidence trickster. The autobiographies of the great magicians, for example those of Herrmann, Carl Hertz and Horace Goldin, are full of stories of how they turned the tables on shysters. I'm afraid I disbelieve most of their stories of such exploits, though I admit they make good reading. In his book: *Modern Mystery Merchant*, Carl Hertz tells a story of three card-sharps engaging him in a game on a train. He explains how he used his magical knowledge and won all their money. Can you imagine a hard-bitten gang of card-sharps allowing a harmless, respectable showman to cheat *them* at cards?

If you give a pack of cards, a nice new pack freshly unwrapped, to a crooked gambler, he will dream of the people he can fleece with it. But give the same pack to a conjurer and he will dream of all the pleasure and entertainment that it will help him to create. His fingers will itch to caress and manipulate the pasteboard, as he admires anew the beautiful designs of the court cards. Playing cards really are attractive, and in the hands of a good manipulator they become even more so. There are two ways in which the conjurer can use the cards. He can present with them tricks of the 'take a card . . . put it back . . . here it is' variety. Or he can manipulate the cards to show his skill. This kind of act is usually presented in silence, to melodic background music. The manipulator will produce card after card, even fan after fan of cards, seemingly from mid-air. Then he will make pleasing designs with the pack, and perhaps throw in some fancy cuts and shuffles. Although this is more akin to juggling than conjuring, the two arts blend well.

Such a fine, sophisticated act was presented by one of the best remembered of all magicians, Cardini. His character, that of gentleman who has had a little too much champagne, trying to perform with cards, became the most widely imitated in the history of show business. Born in Wales in 1899, as Richard Valentine Pitchford, he served as a very young soldier in France during the 1914–18 war. In the trenches, in the bitter winter of 1917, he had been obliged to wear gloves when practising his card manipulations. After the war he continued to wear gloves, but silk ones, and his audience gave him more applause than they would have if he had worked bare-handed. Under the name Val Raymond he conjured his way round the world, but did not gain fame until he became the bland, monocled Cardini. When he played the London Palladium Theatre in 1937, he performed in front of a set of blue velvet curtains, known to this day as the 'Cardini blues'. That's fame!

Those same blue drapes were used again for an American

Fig. 24. **Cardini** – one of the world's greatest sleight-of-hand magicians. *From the Houdini files in the Davenport Collection.*

magician in 1955, Channing Pollock. Opening with card-manipulations, much as Cardini had done, Pollock went on to produce doves, from innocent silk squares. This delighted an audience that had previously only seen doves produced from elaborate boxes and bags. His became the second most imitated act, and soon it seemed as if every conjurer, amateur or professional, was producing doves in that way. But it did not bother Channing Pollock as he soon stopped being a magician and became a film actor.

Of course acts like those of Cardini and Channing Pollock can be easily seen and appreciated, even in the largest theatres. One would imagine that there would be little scope in such places for conjurers of the 'take a card' variety. After all, only the first half-dozen rows of the audience could actually recognise the card faces. Yet a balding, bearded gentleman, Billy O'Connor, with the suavity of his French father, and the blarney of his Irish mother, worked such tricks in the largest auditoriums. He would walk out onto a huge stage, with nothing but a pack of cards, and say: 'I don't want to cause any ill-feeling, but I'm next!' His impish charm and personality made the fact that most of the audience could not see the card faces unimportant. He billed his act as 'Billy O'Connor and His Fifty-Two Assistants'. Once, in Australia, he arrived at a theatre to find that chorus dressing-rooms had been provided for his 'company'. The manager was surprised to learn that the fifty-two assistants were pasteboard.

Tricks with coins have been popular almost since coinage began. Several magicians have been celebrated for their manipulation of the silver discs, none more so than T. Nelson Downes, born in rural Iowa in 1867. He worked as a railway booking-office clerk, which gave him much opportunity to handle coinage. By the turn of the century however, he had become well known in American vaudeville as the King of Koins. A feature of his work was the very deliberate way in which he manipulated the silver dollars. There was no question of the quickness of the hand. Eventually he had his own coins minted, with the Downes head in place of that of a monarch. He would throw some of the coins to members of the audience, as he produced them. These coins, where they still exist, are prized collectors' items.

During the 1930s there was a great vogue for magicians to produce, vanish and otherwise manipulate lighted cigarettes. Cardini, Deveen and Frakson, to name a few, would pluck lit cigarettes from the air. Audiences were impressed, for it seemed unlikely that the cigarettes could have been concealed about the persons of the conjurers without tell-tale smoke or smouldering. After producing a dozen lit cigarettes, Cardini would materialise a lit cigar, and finally a furiously smoking meerschaum pipe! In recent years this type of work has been hardly seen at all, and it may be that the campaign to suppress smoking has something to do with it.

As we have discussed, the expression 'the quickness of the hand' is not so valid as would be supposed when applied to the magician or conjurer. But the 'quickness of the mind' is a phrase that can be suitably used to describe the professional mind-reader or 'mentalist'.

Nomad fortune-tellers of Europe, India, China and North Africa were often capable of some 'sleight of mind'.

Some years ago an elderly Indian knocked at my door and informed me that he could see 'the sign of the tiger' on my brow. He gave me a square of paper and asked me to write a number upon it, without showing him what I had written. I was then to fold the paper, rather as would be done with a voting-slip, and hand it to him. He tore the paper to small pieces which scattered, and placing a hand to his brow told me, correctly, the number that I had written. He had used a subterfuge of the professional mind-reader, a secret that could have been handed down, in his family, for centuries. I bought from him a tie that I did not want.

At what point then did the stage mind-reader develop, using tricks evolved by the gypsies and other nomads? Certainly during the mid nineteenth century both Robert-Houdin and Anderson were utilising two-person 'codes', allowing the performer to convey information openly to his partner. A subtle 'double-talk' allowed the conjurer to convey the name of a person or object to the blindfolded 'medium'. 'What is this pray?' 'It's a watch!' 'Please tell me quickly what this is?' 'It is a wallet!' The codes became sophisticated, so that tone of voice as well as actual words could convey so much.

The two-person mind-reading act is seen today only as a

satire by comedians. But in the past there was a great and genuine interest in acts of this kind. The most famous of these teams were the Zancigs, Julius and Ada, billed as 'Two Minds With But a Single Thought'. Zancig was a metal-smelter in his native Sweden, until an accident forced him to turn his hobby into a profession. The mind-reading act with his wife might have been a precarious way to make a living, but it was safer than metal-smelting! So skilled was their demonstration that turn-of-the-century audiences could not be blamed for thinking it to be genuine mind-reading. Sir Arthur Conan-Doyle was convinced of their gift, but then he also believed that Houdini performed his escapes by dematerialising his body!

During their early struggles to establish their act, the Zancigs performed at Hammerstein's roof-garden theatre in New York. They were not a great success until one night, when their act was moved to the last on the programme. Today of course, the final act on a show is usually the star, but until fairly recently a variety show would always have an act to follow that of the star, during which most of the audience would walk out. These acts were known as 'chasers', and were useful, because when several performances a day were given it was important to clear the theatre of people as quickly as possible. But this insult was in the Zancigs' favour. With fewer people in the theatre, Julius walked on and implored those who remained to move nearer the stage. With an intimate atmosphere created, he and Ada captivated the small audience. Their legend had begun, and soon they were famous. When Ada died, Julius married another lady, Agnes, who was willing to spend the months, even years, involved with learning the code. Eventually the Zancigs reappeared on the theatre circuits, but were never as perfect as the original act had been.

The solo mind-reading act or 'mentalist' is one of the most difficult forms of magic to present with conviction. For not only must the mentalist have a first-class repertoire, but he must be a good showman, and the audience must know of his powers through publicity before they enter the theatre. Such a man was Maurice Fogel. He had, in his youth, served a hard apprenticeship as a 'spieler', outside the Southend side-show of the illusionist Rameses. The job of a spieler was to attract an audience to the show. But due to the supposed Egyptian's fondness for the bottle, Maurice often had to perform the show inside as well! Later he managed to get onto all the best theatre circuits as a solo mind-reading act, following a not too successful period as a magician. Of short stature and stocky build, Fogel was one of the outstanding showmen of the twentieth century. He could raise an audience to great enthusiasm, and quell a heckler with a dry remark or even just an expressive glance. He told people how much change they had in their pockets, the names of their long-dead relatives, and could predict, by writing on a slate, the very word that they would choose from thousands in a book. Lion-headed, with an expression of great thoughtfulness, Maurice always had a good story for the press. One of these, concerning his performance of the bullet-catching trick, got him banner headlines. Maurice claimed that on one occasion he had not only caught the bullet in his teeth, but accidentally swallowed it. He had hospital X-rays to prove it! When Fogel died in 1981, I felt that we had seen the last of the great, exciting showmen in the Houdini mould. He died of a heart attack at Golders Green underground station, on his way to a performance. He was about sixty-eight years old, his date of birth being as much a mystery as his amazing feats.

Al Koran was another solo mind-reader, famous during the fifties and sixties. The silver-haired ex-commando and one-time hairdresser came to fame through a television series in the mid fifties. Although he did not invent the mysteries around which his act was built, Al got a great name among magicians for originality, because of his talent to take a very old or simple feat and dress it up to be a modern miracle. His ability to make much out of a little is perhaps illustrated by the following story:

Al was invalided from the forces in 1944, and he and his wife Kay went to live in a small flat in east London. When I visited them I commented on the wonderful job that Al had made of furnishing and decorating a flat at a time of great shortage of almost everything. I particularly admired the handsome clock that stood on the mantlepiece. Al grinned, turned the cabinet round, and showed me the works. Unable to afford or obtain such a clock, Al had constructed a wooden case which he had polished and varnished. He had then cut a hole in the centre of the cabinet, and placed a cheap utility alarm-clock behind it.

The alarm-clock was set on blocks to keep it in position, and nobody would have known that it was not the handsome article it appeared to be.

He died in the United States in 1972. Although only in his fifties, he had written numerous magic books, and a best-seller for the public entitled *Bring Out the Magic in Your Mind*. It was Al's ambition to appear at the London Palladium, but he never appeared there in life. However, through one of his final requests, a friend of his scattered his ashes in the auditorium of that famous theatre, secretly, during a performance!

Today public opinion is rather against the serious presentation of a mind-reading act. We have reached the stage where such harmless chicanery is suspect. It reminds me of the time when Uri Geller first presented his metal-bending on British television. A host of conjurers leapt into the spotlight to expose and ridicule him. I could not see what harm had been done, and I said to one of his attackers: 'If you had thought of it before he did, you would have done it yourself!'

It may no longer be fashionable to believe in miracles, but it is not for me to criticise this trend. Let me just say that *The Arabian Nights* never did me any harm, and many an elderly lady has been greatly comforted by a fortune-teller.

But magic, the art of illusion, is still beyond reproach, and will continue to be popular with audiences as long as people want to be intrigued and entertained. It has been said that modern technology has made the illusionist's art obsolete. Had this been so, the ventriloquist would have gone out of business with the invention of Edison's phonograph. We all know that trick camera-work can produce sensational illusions, but its use would defeat the whole object of the exercise. No machine will ever take a coin from its pocket and make it disappear for the pleasure of a child. At least, not with the style and class with which a magician can do it!

Easy card tricks for you to perform

Card tricks are popular with audiences, and are a natural thing for the magician to present. After all, almost every household has at least one pack of playing cards. If the conjurer uses his host's pack, he is likely to be more impressive than if he used his own, which people might suspect of being faked or doctored. The tricks which follow are simple ones, which can be presented with any pack of cards.

Although it is important to be able to handle and shuffle the cards in a competent manner, without dropping them all over the floor, no attempt should be made to indulge in fancy or stagey moves with them. There is little advantage in trying to show off a skill with the cards, when the effects are supposed to be gained through 'magic', rather than dexterity. This is not to suggest that the performer truly expects his audience to believe in supernatural powers, as did the magicians of centuries past. But no advantage is gained by going to an opposite extreme.

In case you should be tempted to believe that some of the tricks which follow are too simple, let me persuade you otherwise. The trick known as 'Three Pile Divination' I once saw presented by Orson Welles to a rapt audience. Of course the actor's powerful personality would have made an entertainment out of the twice-times-table, but he illustrated to me that any trick, however simple, can be made both puzzling and entertaining if presented in the right way. Welles created an air of mystery which soon had the audience under his spell.

Three Pile Divination

The magician shuffles the pack of cards and carelessly cuts it into three piles, which he places side by side on the table. Although it would seem impossible, from the audience's view-point, he correctly names the top card of each pile. The trick can be performed with a borrowed pack of cards.

When you have learned how the trick is accomplished you may well accuse me of a misleading description. Yet I can assure you that if the trick is smartly performed, members of the audience will later describe it as I have done!

In shuffling the pack, take careful note of the card that is on top of the pack. You can do this very easily by first running through the pack and enquiring: 'Does the pack have jokers?' In so doing, note mentally the top card, and shuffle the pack in a way that does not disturb it from that position. (Expert card manipulators call this a false-shuffle, and have a dozen different ways to do it. But I think it will be found easy enough to shuffle the pack without moving that top card.)

Cut the pack into three piles. You are now aware of the card that is on the top of one of the piles, but have no idea, any more than the audience have, of the cards on the tops of the other two piles. But you use that one small piece of knowledge in a crafty way. Let us assume that the card you know is at the top of the pile to your left, and that it is the ace of clubs.

Point to the pile to your right, and announce that the card on the top of that pile is the ace of clubs (or whatever card it is that you already know). Remove it from the top of the pile, glance at it, smile as if in triumph, but do not show it to the spectators. Let us assume that the card is in fact the two of diamonds. Point to the centre pile and announce that the top card is the two of diamonds. Remove it, glance at it, as before, but do not show it to anyone. We will assume that it is the four of spades. One pile remains to be dealt with, the right-hand pile with the known ace of clubs on top of it. Point to that top card and name it as the four of spades. Remove it, glance at it and smile triumphantly. You now have three cards in your hand, which you have seemingly named before seeing them, as the ace of clubs, the two of diamonds and the four of spades. Those are the three cards that you are holding . . . only their order is in doubt. So throw them carelessly, face up, on the table, so that they are no longer in the order that they were picked up.

This neat trick is based on a principle known as

'one ahead'. If you perform it smartly, without pausing to allow any interruption between naming and picking up the cards, it will fool everyone. The only way you can fail with it is if you hesitate after picking up a card that you have named. A long pause would be the perfect cue for someone to say, 'Let me see it'. If anyone even looks as if he is about to speak during your performance of the trick, hold up an admonishing hand, as if to say 'don't stop me from concentrating'! (Or even say it, if the gesture is not enough.) It is important that the trick is presented with flow and style. When the climax has been reached and while they are still gasping, pick up the cards, shuffle the pack, and start in on another trick. Avoid allowing them to discuss what you have done.

The Mystic Seven

The magician arranges three piles of cards on the table, each pile being obviously composed of a different number of cards. He writes a 'prediction' on a piece of paper, which is folded and given to a spectator to place in his pocket. Another spectator is asked to choose any of the three piles of cards, and it is clear that he has an absolutely free choice. The prediction is unfolded and proves to be correct. It reads: 'You will choose the seven pile.'

Whichever of the three piles of cards has been chosen this prediction *has* to be correct. The first pile consists of four sevens. The second pile consists of seven cards. The third pile consists of cards where the total number of pips involved adds up to seven (e.g. ace, two and four; or three aces and two twos). If the pile with the four sevens is selected, fine, and be sure to show the faces of the cards in the other piles. If the second pile, the one which consists of seven cards, is chosen, do not show the faces of any of the cards, just count the number of cards in each heap, to show that the chosen heap is the only seven-card one. If the third heap is chosen, hand it to an intelligent spectator, to total the pips. Then show the faces of the cards in the other heaps, to show that their totals are not seven.

This is possibly the simplest of all card tricks to perform: but additional points of finesse will add to the mystery. For example, it would not be a good idea to be seen arranging the cards carefully before presenting the trick. The best plan is to arrange all the cards required on top of the pack before you start. For example, if you know that the top four are the four sevens, you can deal those four straight down, in a heap. Next your seven cards can be dealt into a heap beside them. Whatever arrangement of cards you have made to add up to seven should follow: but you must remember the number of cards involved, to be able to deal them. Practice the use of this little 'set-up', and it will add to the effect, allowing you to deal the heaps with seemingly carelessness.

An easy 'find the lady' trick

If you are presenting a few magic tricks, sooner or later someone is certain to enquire if you can show them the famous 'three-card trick'. The version which follows can be performed with an absolute minimum of sleight of hand.

Three cards are fanned, and the audience can see that the card in the centre of the fan is a queen. The fan is closed, and the cards are placed face down on the table. No matter how hard they try, the audience cannot 'find the lady'. For a finale, the three cards can be turned over, to show that they are all spot cards, the queen having entirely vanished.

Preparation: There are three spot cards, plus a queen, which is really a 'pocket' to fit over the corner of one of the spot cards. This pocket can be made by cutting two matching corners from a queen and any other card. Sellotape hinges hold the two card fragments together, and the pocket should be fitted to the corner

75

of the centre card, and the three cards held in a fan as illustrated in Diagram 1.

Performance: Show the fan, with the queen quite obviously in the centre. Close the fan as in Diagram 2, turn the cards, backs up, and place them in the left hand (see Diagram 3). Draw the cards, one at a time, from the left hand, with the fingers of the right. Lay them in a row, move them around, they simply cannot find the queen, because the pocket has been left in your left hand.

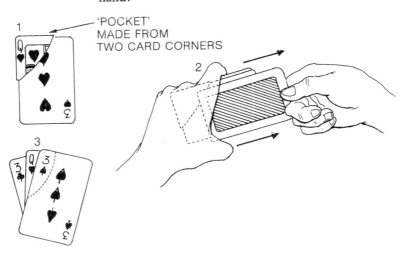

'POCKET' MADE FROM TWO CARD CORNERS

The mysterious ace

Here is a simple trick which, if well presented, will give the appearance of sleight of hand, yet requires no skill to present. Three cards are shown in a fan, the aces of clubs, diamonds and spades. They are closed up and placed in the centre of the pack, which is then stood face down on the table. The top card is turned over, and proves to be the very ace of diamonds that was placed in the centre. The cards are scattered around, face up, so that the audience can see that no duplicate cards are involved.

Performance: The card held in the centre of the fan, appearing to be the ace of diamonds is in fact the ace of hearts, arranged as illustrated, with the two other cards masking part of it, to give the impression of a diamond. The rest is obvious. The real ace of diamonds is already on top of the pack, and the scattering at the end will separate the three aces at the centre.

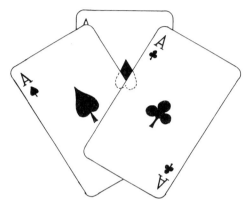

A quick change

The magician places a playing-card into a glass tumbler. He makes sure that everyone is certain of its face value. Then he covers the glass with a handkerchief. He asks one of the people watching to name the card in the glass. But when he whisks the handkerchief away a quite different card rests in the glass. The handkerchief can be a borrowed one.

Preparation: Have any card in the pack reversed.

Performance: Take from the pack the card which has the reversed card next to it; but bring the reversed card out with it. These cards are in fact back to back, but of course this fact should not be known to the spectators who think that a single card is being held. The two cards, held as one, are placed in a glass tumbler (see Diagram 1).

77

The audience should still think that a single card is there. In covering the glass with a handkerchief, give the vessel a turn (Diagram 2), so that the other card now faces the audience, although they are unaware of any change. The rest is obvious. Simply whisk away the handkerchief. There is a completely different card. Audiences will usually suspect the handkerchief, so it is as well to borrow one. In returning the handkerchief, and allowing the people to look at it, take the opportunity to lift the two cards from the glass, and slip them into the pack.

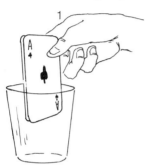

BACK TO BACK
CARDS, HELD
'AS ONE'
PLACED INTO
GLASS

R. HAND TURNS GLASS
AS L. HAND DRAPES
HANDKERCHIEF OVER IT

Card to chosen pocket

This is a sensational trick, but very easy to perform. It requires no skill, just confidence.

The magician has a card selected, and placed on top of the pack. He then asks a spectator to place the back of his left hand on top of the pack and to press down upon his left hand with his right. The magician shows him how to do this. The spectator does as asked, and the card is found to have vanished from the top of the pack. The magician finds it in the pocket of a spectator. The person and pocket can be specified by the audience.

Preparation: You need to moisten the back of your left hand just before performing the trick. Have the card selected and placed on top of the pack, which should be placed upon the table. Explain to one of the people that you want him to place the back of his left hand on the top of the pack, and to press down upon that hand with his right. Show him how to do this by placing the moistened back of your own left hand on the pack, and pressing down on it as in the illustration. When you remove your hands, the top card will stick to the damp back of your left hand. Place your hands smartly behind your back, and transfer the card to the palm of your right hand. The spectator does as you have done, and is told then to look through the pack. The chosen card is of course no longer to be found, as it is concealed in your right hand. Let the people choose a person, and name which of his pockets they would like the card to be found in. Place your right hand smartly into that pocket, and 'produce' the card from it.

MOISTENED BACK OF LEFT HAND IN CONTACT WITH TOP CARD

Unlike the conjurer who 'palms' a card away from the pack, you have all the time in the world to arrange that card carefully in your right palm, so there is little fear of detection.

The four aces

The mysterious assembly of the four aces is a popular trick with magicians, who have a hundred different ways of performing the feat, in most cases requiring skill and a great deal of practice. But here is an easy and quickly learned method of doing the same thing. The effect upon an audience will be the same anyway. So why do the magicians indulge in all those difficult sleight of hand moves to do it? If I could answer that question I could settle a fifty-year-long argument!

The magician shows the four aces fanned in his hand. On the table lies the rest of the pack. The fan of aces is closed and the cards placed, face down, on top of the pack. The top card, the first ace, is removed, and its face is shown. It is placed aside on the table. The second ace, logically now the top card, is placed underneath the pack. The third ace, now the top card, is taken and inserted about two-thirds of the way down, in the pack. The top card now is the last ace. This is removed and inserted about half-way down the pack. The ace which has been placed aside is again shown, and placed, face down on top of the pack. The aces have been distributed fairly evenly through the pack. But the magical climax occurs when the magician produces the four aces from the top of the pack. All the cards can be examined.

Preparation: When the fan is seen, it appears to be of the four aces: and so it is, except that behind the second ace three other (any) cards are held, as in the illustration.

Performance: The fan is closed, the heap of cards, seemingly four but in fact seven, is placed on top of the pack. The top card really is an ace, and is placed aside. The next three cards are of course not aces, and these are distributed through the pack as already explained. The climax is an easy and effective one, with the real aces taken from the top of the pack and shown. Care should be taken not to show the faces of other cards when placing them at different points in the pack.

A little practice is required before one can convincingly show and fan the aces, with the concealed cards behind one of them.

These three cards are actually concealed behind the Ace of Diamonds but have been shown in an exaggerated position for sake of clarity.

Chapter 6
The magic of India

Westerners have always regarded the Indian mystics and fakirs with some awe. In days gone by a side-show charlatan had only to don a turban and a robe to give even the most mediocre magical performance some mysterious flavour. It is interesting to note that the great illusionists have tended to dismiss the native Indian magicians as being vastly overrated, yet almost all of them have dressed up portions of their shows in an Indian style. They have said, 'Western magic is far better,' but in so saying I feel that they have perhaps failed to judge the performance of the Indian conjurer fairly. One has to consider the effect that it has on the audiences for which it is designed. You cannot try to make comparison between the itinerant street conjurer or 'jadoo wallah' and the sophisticated European magician who has the advantage of stage facilities and skilled craftsmen. But before going any further, it is worth examining a performance by an Indian street conjurer, bearing in our mind its traditions, and that it could have been given, as described, a month or several centuries ago.

The scene is a street-market in a large city midway between Bombay and Calcutta in 'the land of a thousand mysteries'. There are sellers of food, birds in cages, and water-vendors. Tethered goats bleat as they are jostled by a noisy and colourful crowd. Suddenly there arrives on the scene an elderly man, wearing the voluminous loin cloth and green turban of his kind. He is Carim, jadoo wallah and local wonder-worker. His boy assistant carries his properties in a large circular basket.

Carim's first job is to spread out his properties in the correct manner for performance. But he wastes nothing, using these actions to attract a crowd, singing his mysterious incantations as he works. Then, with all the items arranged to his liking, he takes up a pipe made from a gourd, and starts to play a melancholy tune. The people draw nearer. He squats, still playing the pipe, and seeing the circular basket, strangers could be forgiven for believing him to be a snake-charmer. But the basket is a little large and the pipe quite wrong for such a performance. The boy places a bowl before Carim, and pours water into it from a goatskin bag. This action commands attention, for water is of very great value and not to be treated lightly. Carim picks up and displays to the crowd a small carved wood duck, of the kind used by hunters as a decoy. He floats the toy duck on the water in the bowl and begins to play again on the pipe. The duck circles the bowl, as if alive, then Carim ceases to play and the duck stops circling. He commands it to sink, and it does so, but it reappears on the surface of the water when he tells it to. This is repeated a number of times, for the benefit of those who have just joined the crowd, and then the water is poured back into the skin bag for future use.

There is much muttering, exclamations of amazement and a little laughter from the crowd, though of course many of them have seen the feat before, Carim being a local favourite. He unwinds the turban from the head of his boy assistant. His religion prevents him from uncovering his own head in public, but the boy is of lower caste. The turban is held up to show its entire length. The magician cuts it at the centre with a knife, and ties the two pieces together. He drops the untidy ends of the knot in the fire of the sweet-vendor and allows it to smoulder. Suddenly he pulls on the turban, and the remnants of the smouldering knot fall away to show the turban restored. He wraps it back on to the boy's head.

Next, the magician catches a number of coins from nowhere, depositing them in a shallow metal bowl, and referring to them as the boy's wages. Alas, he explains that it is not enough money, but the gods will not allow him to find more coins in the air. He asks the audience to contribute to the boy's pay, passing the bowl round among them for that purpose. While this collection is being made, Carim prepares for his next wonder.

He announces that he will present the wonderful magic mango-tree, which will grow right before their eyes. Thus he breaks the golden rule of the Western magicians, who will never tell the audience what is about to occur. He plants three sticks in the ground, to form a pyramid, and plants a single seed in their midst. He wraps a piece of cloth around the sticks, forming a tiny tent. He plays upon his pipe, waters the area from a tin, and pulls the canvas from the sticks to reveal a small mango shoot. Then Carim builds a fresh tent over the shoot, with larger sticks and bigger canvas. More pipe-playing, watering and incantations. The cloth is pulled away to show a mango-plant, small but unmistakable. He repeats the whole process yet again, to reveal a mango tree, large enough to be bearing fruit!

Next the boy assistant proves rather more cheeky than is good for him, so the magician draws a knife and orders the unfortunate urchin to stick out his tongue. Carim quite deliberately cuts off the protruding portion of the tongue, and makes comedy by addressing the boy and becoming annoyed when he is unable to understand the grunted reply. More comedy when he drops the tongue on the earth, picks it up and cleans it on his loin cloth. He tells the crowd that he will restore the boy's tongue, and in order to do this he applies his own saliva to it, before thrusting it back into the boy's mouth. The boy sticks out his tongue, and members of the crowd can gather round and examine it, proclaiming that the tongue is exactly as it should be. This gruesome effect is acceptable in the setting in which it is presented. The boy has proved to be quite a comedian, his facial activities contributing a great deal to the trick.

Now Carim squats, to present his version of the classic Indian cups and balls. He has three shallow cups, each with a knob on its dome, so that the cups look like pot lids when standing upside-down. The knobs make for the easy movement of the cups when the magician slides the knob between his first and second finger. He makes the three balls vanish, reappear, transpose and generally travel around under the cups. Sometimes he lifts the cups cleanly, and at other times he pushes them forward along the ground before lifting them, in the manner of the Western 'Three Shell Game'.

The magician and his assistant now stage one of their frequent quarrels. The boy hides in the circular basket, pulling its small round lid down over the aperture. He is rather like a lobster caught in a lobster-pot, and the basket looks like a giant version of that article. The magician mimes that he is not able to

84

find the boy, but the crowd soon tell him where the boy is. It is not that they are unkind, it is just that they know their 'cue' from previous performances!

Carim takes up a large metal sword, and with loud cries thrusts it through the basket again and again, at every conceivable angle. Obviously, he explains, there can be no boy in the basket, or his death cries would have been heard. He confirms this by removing the lid and covering the basket with a cloth, which he stamps down into the basket with his bare feet.

The boy being lost, and the sole support of a widowed mother, Carim takes up a collection for that unfortunate woman. When he has collected as much as he can, he replaces the lid on the basket, and the boy reappears, balancing the lid on his head.

Carim will vary this show of course. Sometimes he will have his eyes covered with flour paste, and bound with yards of cambric, yet be able to recognise any object shown to him. He will run his fingers over printed words on paper and speak them aloud. He speaks quite frequently during his performance, yet not in the glib, practised way of a Western conjurer. Sometimes he will make sage comments, such as, 'Carim's enemies criticise his wonders . . . yet entirely fail to explain them!' Although he uses quite modern phrases, he also speaks at times in the English of the King James' Bible.

All of the illusions and tricks described are traditional and have been performed for centuries in India. Most of them have been shown to Western audiences, and have been almost as effective as they would have been in their correct setting. The cut turban and basket tricks have been used with success countless times by European performers in England and America.

P. C. Sorcar, a genuine Indian magician with a huge illusion act, presented the tongue-cutting trick on the stage of London's Duke of York's Theatre in 1955. Some of the audience were offended. His son Sorcar Junior now presents the show, wisely omitting the tongue-cutting feat. But the young Indian magician makes a great deal of the 'X-Ray Eyes' feat, with the dough on his eyes, following the tradition of the jadoo wallahs. Another Indian, Amir Bux, of a famous magic family, made much of the coin catching and cut turban trick for British audiences in the forties and fifties, while his brother Kuda made a complete thirty-minute act from the X-ray vision.

But perhaps the Indian performer longest before the British public was Shek-Ben-Ali, who worked the variety, cabaret and club scenes here for forty years until his death in 1972. The coin-catching was his big feat, and he used a simple tin of the kind used by butchers to hold hearts and livers. His expression, 'Nobody inside . . . nobody outside . . . come Charlie!' which he uttered while showing the tin to be empty became his catch-phrase. He had the lively face and magnetic smile of so many Indians. Instead of bowing to applause, he would salute, like a soldier.

But Europeans impersonating Indian magicians have outnumbered the native performers of this type of act in Britain. In the great days of variety, Gustave Fasola dressed himself and his illusions in Indian style. He used sari-clad young women from Whitechapel and Lambeth to assist him. Later Ali Bey did the same, until seriously injured by a descending safety curtain. Too ill to work, he persuaded the Great Masoni, a magician who owned his own magic revue *Out of the Hat*, to stand in for him. The act was improved by the substitution, for Masoni was a fine showman.

One of the Ali Bey mysteries was *The Girl without a Middle*. The girl, attired as a belly-dancer, would enter, and be placed into a cabinet which was rather like a wide sentry-box. A door was closed, leaving only her head, and the lower half of her legs showing. Then the magician opened the centre door to show that her body had disappeared, and a similar door at the back of the cabinet so that the audience could see right through the apparatus. The magician would walk right around the cabinet, and peer through the space at the audience, proving the absence of those mirrors which so many people are willing to believe in! Murray, the casually effective illusionist from Australia, also featured this illusion, as did Dante, Kalanag, and Thurston. It was invented in 1924 by P. T. Selbit, who presented it with a 'toy soldier' dressing. Some of his other inventions include the 'Human Pincushion' and 'Dividing a Lady'. The latter was a sawing-in-half effect, but it was somewhat eclipsed by Horace Goldin's version, in which the head, hands and feet were in view the whole time. Since Selbit's death in 1939, at the age of

Fig. 25. **P. T. Selbit** (Percy Thomas Tibbles) startled London and the world with the most successful illusion ever invented – 'Sawing a Woman in Two'! *Photo from the Davenport Collection.*

Fig. 26. **Kalanag** – a German illusionist who, with his beautiful assistant Gloria, astounded audiences after World War II with illusions such as 'The Indian Rope Trick'. *From the Davenport Collection.*

fifty-nine, his many illusions have lived on in the hands of other great magicians.

If you were to ask the average person to name a trick or illusion they would be likely to reply 'the Indian Rope Trick'. Yet they might not know if it was fact or fable. Which is it?

The illusion, or fable, as related by many a returning traveller begins in a market-place or open space where a conjurer has performed a traditional show of the kind described in the earlier part of this chapter. The conjurer is then said to ask if anyone in the crowd would like to see a performance of the famous 'Hindu Rope Trick', and if so he would be willing to take them to a place where, far from the hurly-burly of the market, they could behold this wonder. No doubt a certain amount of money would have to change hands before he led a select band of people to some prepared desert area. He would take a long, thick, rope from a basket and allow the company to inspect it. He would replace the rope in the basket and play upon a pipe or flute. The rope then appeared to emerge from the basket, rearing up quite quickly in the direction of the sky. With the rope standing erect, a small boy would climb to the top. After a minute or so, the magician would order the boy to climb down. Far from doing so, the boy would 'disappear', and the rope would quite suddenly descend. That was the end of the story as related by some so-called eye-witnesses.

Other travellers have stated that the magician climbed up the rope after the boy, sword in mouth. Once at the top, he hacked the boy to pieces with the sword, arms, legs, head and trunk dropping to the ground. The magician is supposed then to have placed the parts of the boy into the basket, out of which the boy bounded, quite restored!

Some beholders have said that the effect was performed near to trees, but as many others have said that the trick was performed right away from any helpful cover, constructions or vegetation.

The most amazing part of the whole thing is that this fable has been taken so seriously by scientists and other learned men. All manner of possible explanations have been suggested – goats' vertebrae inside a hollow rope, a bamboo pole disguised as a rope and pushed up through a hole in the ground, even mass hypnotism!

Most of the great illusionists of the past and present have produced stage versions of the rope-trick, and in many cases have filled their souvenir programmes with articles about the illusion. Of course a stage version is a rather different matter from a performance of the type described by travellers.

Challenges to present the trick at Wembley Stadium, Earl's Court or Olympia, under test conditions were issued through the years by Maskelyne, Bertram Mills and the Magic Circle. None have had to pay out. Obviously the illusion is a myth. But how and where did the legend begin? No actual eye-witness has ever been found, and always the story had been told to someone by a friend, or a relative.

Of course *Arabian Nights*-style stories about people and even animals climbing ladders and trees and disappearing into the sky have been coming out of India, Arabia and China for centuries. But the finer points of this particular effect do not appear to have emerged until the second half of the nineteenth century.

In one of his souvenir programmes, I discovered an article by the magician Dante, which I believe pinpoints the start of the legend. Dante was in Australia in 1911, where he was introduced to an old man called Daddy Lyons, who was ninety-two years old. The old fellow had been an advance agent for Kellar and other magicians, and he took up such a post in India for the famous Davenport Brothers. There was a press conference at which one of the brothers told a fantastic story of a child being passed right through a tree trunk by a jadoo wallah. Others present told other stories, equally fantastic. Then it was Lyons' turn. Right off the top of his head he made up a story about a magician making a rope rise, to be climbed by a boy, who disappeared at the top.

The Davenport Brothers toured India in 1877, so some sort of pattern emerges, for it was around that time that the first legendary tales of the 'Indian Rope Trick' started to be told. If what I believe to be true is so, then an off-the-cuff story related by Daddy Lyons has resulted in a century of fantasy and speculation.

Thumb-penetration trick

This seemingly gruesome little trick is quite harmless to the magician, if he takes the minimum of care. The effect is that the magician wraps his thumb with a handkerchief, and seem to thrust several needles through both handkerchief and thumb.

Preparation: You will require a metal thimble that will fit on the end of your thumb, and it will need to have a few holes in it, lined up so that needles can be pushed in one and will emerge through another. You can use any handkerchief, and several long needles. The thimble should be put on the end of the thumb on the right hand, and held, as in Diagram 1 so that it is not observed by the audience.

Performance: Close the fingers over the thimble, and raise the thumb into a 'thumbs-up' position (Diagrams 2 and 3). Borrow a handkerchief, or extract your own from a pocket with the left hand. In the action of covering the thumb with the handkerchief, insert the thumb into the thimble, and bring it up under the handkerchief, so that its shape will suggest the thumb (Diagram 4).

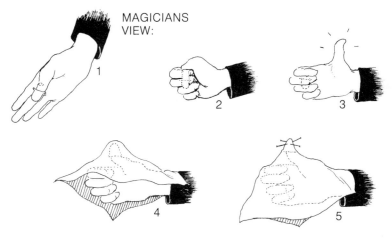

MAGICIANS VIEW:

Keep the thumb low, with the thimble sticking up, and wrap the handkerchief around it. By trial and error you will be able to push through the needles (Diagram 5). (If you are slow with this it will only build up tension.)

To bring the trick to a conclusion, simply withdraw the needles and take the thimble away under cover of the handkerchief. All attention will be on your thumb, which must resume a thumbs-up position.

Mind reading tricks

There is a great deal in the manner in which you should present mind-reading tricks to an audience. Remember, your own mind is supposed to be responsible for the magic, so look thoughtful, and try to create an atmosphere of suspense. One good thing about this branch of magic is that if you fail occasionally no one will think it strange.

International mind reading

Preparation: You will need a sheet of notepaper, a hat and a handkerchief, plus a pen or pencil for the writing of the names. The paper should be folded, ready to tear into three equal pieces.

Performance: The mind-reader takes a sheet of paper and tears it neatly into three pieces. Handing a piece to a spectator he requests him to write the name of a famous French personality on it, and to fold it and place it into a hat. A second spectator is given a piece, and told to write on it the name of an American personality, and to fold it in the same style as the first person, also depositing it in the hat. One other piece, the last one, gets a British name, famous or infamous, written on it. This last piece is also folded and dropped in the hat. Bear in mind that all this has been done in such a way that the performer could not have seen the written names.

Now he is blindfolded with a borrowed handkerchief, and yet he will always pick out from the hat the piece of paper bearing the American name! How does he do this?

When the mentalist asks for the French name to be written, he tears off the first strip, the top third of the paper. The American name is written on the sheet from the middle of the paper, and the English name on the remaining sheet. This means that the American name can easily be detected, by touch, even when the three equal-sized strips are folded in an identical manner, by touch. The blindfolded mentalist simply feels the edges of each folded strip. The one he is looking for will have both its edges slightly serrated by the tear. The others will be perfectly clean-cut on one edge.

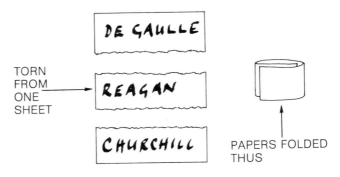

TORN FROM ONE SHEET

PAPERS FOLDED THUS

Although the piece with the two slightly rough edges can be very quickly and easily found, it is important that the mentalist does not find it *too* soon. He or she should hold each folded paper to the forehead in turn, more than once, before announcing the American name. Although this is such a simple secret, you will be amazed at the theories that will be advanced by the average company, regarding the method. Just smile at them mysteriously and say, 'Of course, it might be mind-reading!'

Colour divination

In this splendid little experiment the mentalist gives three crayon pencils to the audience to look at: one red, one blue and one green. He asks someone to select a crayon, and hand it to him behind his back. The mentalist not only correctly names the chosen coloured-pencil, but repeats the experiment successfully.

Preparation: Three full-length coloured pencils, or crayon-pencils.

Performance: When the pencil is handed to the mentalist behind his back, he makes a small mark with it on his right thumb-nail. Holding the pencil still, in his left hand, he brings the right hand up to his forehead, in a gesture of concentration. In doing so, he is careful to do two things: first, to let the audience see that he is not concealing anything in his hand, and second, to notice the colour of the tiny mark on his right thumb-nail.

The longer the pencils are, the better. You will not be suspected of palming a pencil in the right hand. Perhaps the simplest trick in this book, yet possibly the most effective.

Chapter 7
Magical classics

In music, a work is not a classic when it is written, but becomes one if over the years it is often to be heard. In magic there are classics, classic tricks and classic illusions that have stood the test of time, as for example the cups and balls. The same can be said about the 'Chinese Rings'.

What other tricks and illusions are classics, and why?

One which immediately comes to mind is the 'Egg Bag'. In his *Modern Magic* published in 1875, Professor Hoffman tells us that the 'Egg Bag' is a very old-fashioned trick. He suggests that it was introduced to London 'some years ago' by a troupe of Japanese jugglers. Well, the specification that Hoffman gives (an eight-inch square bag, prepared in a certain way, and an egg), is accurate in describing the apparatus as it is used today, but the trick that he describes with it is completely different.

I think Albini must have been the first magician to realise the immense possibilities of these simple properties. With their aid he first produced an egg from a seemingly empty bag. He then told his audience that he would cause the egg to vanish from the bag. He placed it therein, and withdrew his hand in a very suspicious manner, culminating with a movement to his left armpit. He showed the bag to be empty, which did not surprise the audience, because they firmly believed that the egg was under his left arm. When there were cries of 'Lift your arms!' he raised his right arm. He then lifted his left arm but only from the elbow. When the heckling that this produced was at its height, he raised the left arm completely and produced the egg from the bag. He next invited two spectators from the audience onto the stage, and allowed one to stand to each side of him as he placed the egg again in the bag. He made the egg once more vanish, and allowed each man to feel inside the bag, without finding it. He screwed the bag into a small bundle, opened it out

Fig. 27. **Jean-Eugene Robert-Houdin** (1805–71) – the man regarded as the father of modern magic.

Fig. 28. Robert-Houdin's famous levitation 'Suspended Equilibrium'.

Fig. 29. **Robert-Houdin** performing with his son in an act in which the boy described objects submitted by spectators.

again, placed flat on the floor and even trampled on it. He picked up the bag, and instructed each man to hold one of his wrists tightly. While still holding the wrists they were allowed 'one last feel inside the bag'. Then, under these completely impossible conditions, one of the men was told to 'Look inside'. The egg was back in the bag!

When Horace Goldin was a young magician he was told by other performers of the great brilliance of Albini with this particular trick. He traced the heavy-drinking magician to a New York bar, and hired him to teach him the routine. Whatever it cost it was money well spent, because it got Goldin out of many a tight spot. Through the years he became even more expert with the 'Egg Bag' than his tutor had been, and with his Polish accent, it made a nice and amusing change in his act from the whirlwind of silent magic in which he specialised. When he entertained Edward VII, Queen Alexandra and the Kaiser at Sandringham he was warned to leave it out of his programme because it was known that during his presentation he removed his tailcoat, to avoid suspicion of concealment of the egg. Goldin got excited, performed the trick, and removed the coat. Obviously he did not offend royalty in so doing, for they were lavish in their praise of this particular trick. Despite his accent, his stammer, his homely features and very ample build, he had great charm and a lovely smile.

Another great magician, also an illusionist in the grand manner, who used the 'Egg Bag' as an effective quiet interlude was Arnold de Biere. He had a very delicate touch with the trick, and took the trouble to use a blown egg rather than the ivorine imitation favoured by most magicians. This meant that he must take great care not to damage the egg, but the bag would have that lightness when held by a spectator that an empty bag should have. A true artist.

Cecil Lyle, another fine illusionist, featured the 'Egg-Bag', following the Goldin tradition. Lyle had a gimmick with it. He had the egg signed by every celebrity who assisted him in the trick. Film starts, cabinet ministers and great sportsmen had signed it. Lyle explained to the audience that the egg was his most treasured possession, and that he would not want to lose it. 'I do . . . every night . . . but it always comes back!' he quipped.

Of the classic stage illusions, perhaps the so called 'Box Trick' of J. N. Maskelyne is the most celebrated. Maskelyne was born in Cheltenham in 1839. He was already an amateur conjurer when he attended a performance by the Davenport Brothers at the Cheltenham Town Hall in March 1865. It should be made clear that the Davenports claimed actual supernatural aid when objects which they placed in a curtained cabinet became animated. Maskelyne, who had stepped up from the audience to assist the brothers, happened to spot their deception. He felt it his duty to inform the audience about this. However, led by a clergyman, they shouted him down. So in order to prove that he was right, Maskelyne staged his own demonstration, duplicating all the effects of the Davenports, assisted by his friend George Cooke. The performance was given at Jessops Gardens on 19 June 1865, where Maskelyne was careful to inform the audience that everything was effected by natural means. An aspect of this business of tricks becoming classic is that nearly all of the items thought by most to be classical are perhaps more than a hundred years old. Some of

Fig. 30. **Cecil Lyle**, one of Britain's leading illusionists after the Second World War. *Photo from the Davenport Collection.*

Fig. 31. Poster showing Cecil Lyle performing his amazing illusion 'Find the Lady'. *From the Davenport Collection.*

Fig. 32. **John Neville Maskelyne** (1839–1917) – the father of British magic and the founder of the Maskelyne dynasty of magicians which lasted from 1865 to 1933, when his last theatre, St George's Hall, closed in London.

Fig. 33. One of the magnificent programmes from St George's Hall. *From the Davenport Collection.*

them even go back for thousands of years. But is this not the same with music? There are numbers known as evergreens, meaning that they are popular numbers which refuse to drop out of favour. Such a trick is 'The Six-Card Repeat', so called because the conjurer counts six cards, throws away three and still has six. He repeats this process several times. Invented by American magician, Tommy Tucker, in 1934, the trick was immensely popular with conjurers and soon it was impossible to see a magician without seeing this trick! Then, about ten years ago, the trick was obviously far too well known and it was dropped from everyone's repertoire. Recently, a magician revived it on television, and now everyone is performing it again. It's a true evergreen, though obviously it will have its revivals at regular intervals over the years.

So successful was the performance that the two young men from Cheltenham toured Great Britain. Naturally, Maskelyne had to expand his repertoire, so soon, in addition to the spirit-cabinet demonstration, and Maskelyne's small tricks and plate-spinning, they introduced the famous 'Box Trick'. The box, which was the forerunner of the trunk and box illusions used later by Houdini and many another, was based upon an effect usually performed by Indian magicians with a large wicker hamper. Maskelyne's box was of solid polished wood and brass bound. He could be locked inside it, and the box placed behind a curtain, and he would be free within seconds. He and Cooke sometimes changed places, with Cooke appearing in the box into which Maskelyne had been locked.

They successfully toured the provinces for some eight years before the fortunate opportunity of a three-month tenancy of the theatre in the Egyptian Hall in Piccadilly, London, presented itself. The building, with its exotic façade of columns and sphinxes, had been a museum. Maskelyne realised that he could establish there a permanent theatre of mystery, which is just what he did, with Maskelyne and Cooke's eventually becoming as much of a tourist attraction as the Zoo at Regent's Park. Of course in this setting, the magician needed to mount a more spectacular show, and this he did, incorporating his famous 'Box Trick' into a long-running playlet, entitled *Will the Witch and the Watchman*. This sketch incorporated a number of transpositions of the characters, with their mysterious

Fig. 34. Fergus Roy with the original Maskelyne illusion, invented by P. T. Selbit, 'Through the Eye of a Needle'. The steel plate in front weights 90 lbs and the assistant is 'pulled' through this. The head shown is a reproduction of Mary Maskelyne's head made for the collection. *From the Davenport Collection.*

Fig. 35. **The Egyptian Hall**, London (c. 1903). Founded by J. N. Maskelyne and George A. Cooke, this was the home of British magic from 1873 to 1904. *Photo from the Davenport Collection.*

Fig. 36. A programme from the Egyptian Hall. *From the Davenport Collection.*

EPPS'S THE MOST NUTRITIOUS COCOA.

THE
EGYPTIAN HALL, LONDON.
ENGLAND'S HOME OF MYSTERY.

MESSRS

Maskelyne

and Cooke's

ENTERTAINMENT.

28th Consecutive Year in London.

PROGRAMME.

PRICE TWOPENCE.

EPPS'S Glycerine Jujubes: Throat & Cough.

appearances and disappearances between a sack, the box and a cabinet. Even a 'Magic Monkey' was involved, even if he was an actor in an ape costume.

Of course in those days, before more sophisticated entertainments existed, the public showed far more interest in such mysteries than would be so today. Newspapers published so-called 'exposés' of Maskelyne's box, and the magician issued challenges regarding its real secret. It is probable that the wily showman had several models of the box, with variations of mechanism, so that the challenge could never be taken up.

Houdini's 'Metamorphosis' was undoubtedly Maskelyne's box in disguise, and the trick formed the basis for a number of others with trunks, boxes and packing-cases.

When Murray, the man who coined the word 'escapology', added the box mystery to his show, he developed a presentation of it which I have not seen bettered for mystery, speed and subtlety. He first had the box and a sack and curtained cabinet thoroughly examined. He then introduced two girls, a blonde and a brunette, both lovely girls but quite distinct from each other. The brunette was placed in the sack, its top secured, and placed inside the box, which was securely locked and placed inside the curtained cabinet. The blonde would then enter the

Fig. 37. Inside **St George's Hall**, Langham Place, London – the home of British magic from 1904 to 1933.

cabinet, showing her head and one shapely leg through the centre split of the curtains. Murray would say: 'If you want to see two fast girls, I've got 'em, just watch this!' The blonde would then withdraw her head, but not her leg. Almost instantly the brunette's head would emerge, and she would step out, the shapely leg having never been out of view. The box would then be dragged from the cabinet, unlocked, and the blonde would be found inside, in the sealed bag!

Today the 'Substitution Trunk' as it is now known, is featured by dozens of popular illusionists and double-acts in a variety of forms. A true classic of illusion.

Curiously enough very few card tricks have become classics. I think this is because in the minds of the audience, the greater number of them, however performed, are thought to be the same trick. If you talk of card tricks to the layman, he will say: 'Is it the one where somebody takes a card, and the conjurer knows which one it is?' This description could encompass at least two hundred entirely different tricks! However, there are one or two card tricks where some other element is present. For example one of the rare classic card effects involves a chosen card rising mysteriously out of the pack. 'Ah,' you may say, 'is that not also the discovery of a selected card?' It is, but it is also a levitation, with the added mystery of the motivation of the rising card. There are more than one hundred different methods that can be employed to bring about the trick. But whichever is used, the effect upon an audience will be the same! Why do conjurers keep inventing new methods for doing old tricks? It is hard to say, but sometimes of course they will find a method which will greatly improve or simplify an effect.

Another card trick which is a classic, and memorable, is that in which each of two spectators are given five cards to hold, which are counted into their hands. The magician makes some of the cards travel from one spectator's hand to that of the other.

Dinner-table tricks

When you have been a guest at a friend's dinner-party, and everything served has been eaten, and the coffee is circulating, is a golden time for you to entertain with some tricks. Everyone will be in a good and receptive mood, and your host or hostess will be delighted if you very casually start to perform a few minor miracles. Of course you can have some of your more impressive tricks in your pocket. But before you get these out, try to perform one or two little tricks with the articles to be found on the table. Your seeming ability to conjure with anything will greatly enhance your reputation. Here are a few suggestions for tricks of this kind.

Vanishing coin in serviette

The trick is effective with a serviette, if one is to hand at the table. But if you are at one of those homes where paper-napkins are used instead, your handkerchief will do.

The after-dinner entertainer places a coin under a serviette. He shows its shape under the centre, and then pulls the serviette smartly away, to show the coin still gripped between his fingers. He repeats this a number of times, until the audience begin to wonder if he will ever do anything. Then suddenly, he pulls the cloth clear and the coin has gone!

Preparation: A serviette or handkerchief and a heavy coin, such as a 50p piece. (Though a 10p piece will do.)

Performance: Diagram 1 shows how the coin should be held between the finger and thumb of the right hand. The left hand places the cloth over it, and draws it clear, by a hanging corner, to show that the coin is still there. After this has been repeated a few times, place the cloth over the coin, one corner first. In drawing the cloth, so that the coin will stick up under the centre, grasp the coin with the fingers and thumb of the left hand and, holding it under the cloth corner, draw it clear, sticking up the right forefinger under the cloth to look as if the coin is still there (see Diagram 2). Now draw away the cloth completely, to show the right

105

hand innocent of the coin. Drop the serviette in your lap, coin and all. Bring it out again a few seconds later, but leave the coin in your lap.

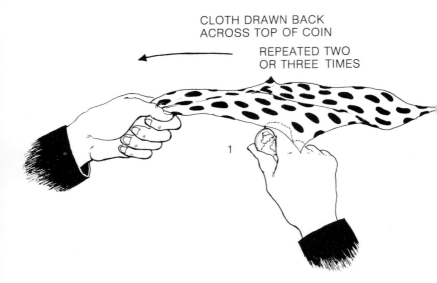

CLOTH DRAWN BACK
ACROSS TOP OF COIN

REPEATED TWO
OR THREE TIMES

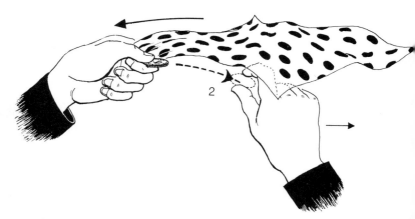

EVENTUALLY, COIN
TAKEN CLEAR BY
FINGERS OF LEFT HAND

The singing wine-glass

A wine glass, filled with any kind of liquid, is made to sing by the magician, simply by waving a fork over it. All he has to do is pluck the prongs of the fork, easy enough, as he waves both hands and a fork over the glass. The resulting 'ping-poing' sound will be thought to be emanating from the liquid if your acting ability is good enough. Don't be in too much of a hurry to pluck the fork.

If you are at the table with one of those people who make glasses sing by damping their fingers and rubbing the glass rim, you have the perfect opportunity to present this little wonder!

Grape stuff

If there is a fruit bowl on the dining table, plus some aerated drink (a not unlikely combination) try the following. Eat a grape, placing the pips on your plate, Pour the aerated beverage into a glass and drop a grape pip into the glass. It will of course sink, but when told, it will rise again to the top of the glass! The carbonated liquid takes care of the whole thing, and causes the pip to rise. All you have to do is 'time' your word of command.

When everyone's attention is elsewhere, secretly take a grape, and hide it in your hand. When attention is not diverted, openly take a grape from the dish in that same hand. Mention that you have 'one grape'. Get someone to hold out a palm, and place the grape on it, closing his fingers over it. But what you really do is place the *two* grapes in his hand. Now take another grape from the dish and eat it. Tell the man holding his hand closed to open it. He now has two grapes . . . the one you placed there, and the one you have just eaten! (At least, that's your story.)

Sympathetic bananas

The effect is that you take two bananas from the fruit dish, open one and cut it into three sections. You explain the sympathy that exists between the two bananas. When you open the second banana, it is already divided into three pieces!

The second banana, previously prepared, was planted on the dish.

Preparation: To prepare such a self-dividing banana, push a needle and thread through the skin at the dividing-point. Guide the needle, so that it goes through most of the thickness of the banana, and emerges about a quarter of an inch from the original hole. Pull out the needle and thread, and repeat the operation further down. Thus, although it will show little or no damage to its skin, the banana when peeled will be almost divided into three.

The magic wand

The magic wand, that symbol of authority and source of mystery, has always played an important part in magic. There have been, through the years, an enormous variety of trick wands constructed especially to appear, disappear, change into flowers or silk, collapse when handed to a helper, or fire a 'flash'. These are all useful, and can often be combined to give brilliant effect. But for our purpose there would be more point in discussing tricks and flourishes that can be performed with a totally unfaked wand. Usually the wand is a stick, made from three-quarter-inch dowel, and decorated in black enamel, with white ends. The purpose of such a wand is to enhance the presentation of a trick. For example, the conjurer wishes to push some handkerchiefs into a tube. It is easier and more artistic to use a wand for the purpose than to try to do it with his fingers. When the conjurer is 'palming' an object, this might be obvious with the hand unoccupied. But if the hand palming the object also holds a wand, the hand will not be suspect.

Another use for the wand is in what the magician calls 'misdirection'. If he wishes to take something from a pocket or elsewhere on his person, without this fact being noticed by the audience, he creates a diversion. He can 'steal' (as he calls it) an object with his left hand while picking up and performing a flourish with the wand with his right hand. This basically is what misdirection means.

Just as a baton is the authority of the musical director, so the wand is the conjurer's symbol of magic. It is very useful to gesture with, in order to draw attention to an object. Rather like the teacher's pointer, the wand increases attention and concentration by the audience.

Of course, if the magician is presenting small tricks at a dinner party or in a friend's living-room, the sudden introduction of this stage-sized wand might cause a raised eyebrow. So I suggest the use of a small wand, if you are going to present small magic. Something nearer to six inches in length, as opposed to the fourteen-inch official symbol, is appropriate. Small wands can be made easily enough or purchased, and this reminds me that the old established magical company, L. Davenport and Co., have recently marketed a ball-pen with the appearance of a magic wand. This looks just like the real thing, but one of the white ends can be removed if you want to use it as a pen. All of the tricks and flourishes, about to be described, can be performed with this handy breast-pocket pen-wand.

The elastic wand

The wonder-worker picks up his wand, large or small, and holding it between a finger and thumb, shakes it. The wand wobbles like india-rubber, but is proved solid. No profound mystery, but a neat little flourish. If you pick up a wand or pencil, and hold it, near to one of its ends, and wobble it up and down, an optical illusion of elasticity is gained. Try it!

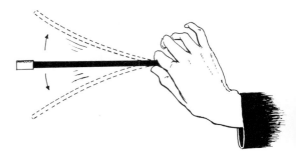

Levitating wand

The magician causes the wand to cling to his fingers as in Diagram 1. Diagram 2 shows how a six-inch ruler, attached by means of his watch-strap is responsible.

The ruler can be pushed up the magician's sleeve to both hide it and release the wand.

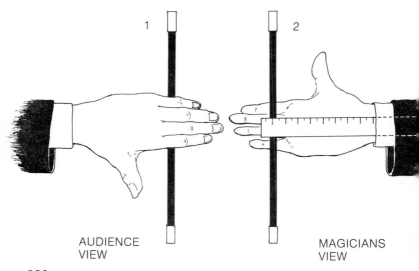

AUDIENCE
VIEW

MAGICIANS
VIEW

Solid through solid

This is a nice little flourish, particularly useful for the conjurer who presents any version of the cups and balls or cups and sponges. It is best with a cup that does not have a handle, and can be used with a glass or plastic tumber, ice-cream carton or picnic cup. The conjurer taps the base of the cup or glass, then pushes the wand right through it. As you will see from the illustration, the wand in fact by-passes the cup, and is thrust between hand and cup. But if it is presented quickly the illusion is perfect. Don't forget to strike the bottom of the cup in one or two preliminary moves, before presenting the flourish.

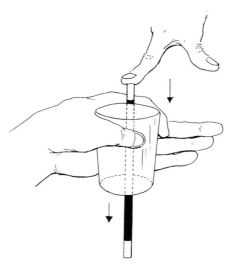

Spinning wand

The wand first sticks to the fingers, and then revolves. As you will see from the diagram, a very small, flesh-coloured rubber-band does the trick. This is worn on the second finger, and will not be noticed either before, during or after the experiment. The conjurer must take an opportunity secretly to wind up the wand, like the propeller on a toy aeroplane.

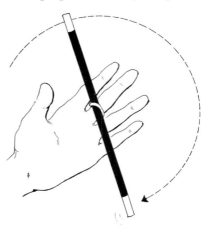

Optical illusions

Most optical illusions are just puzzles, but one or two of them are amazing enough to be presented entertaining as magic tricks. One of these is known these days as the 'Boomerangs'. It has a long history, having been known in the seventeenth century as the 'Funny Noses'.

Two identical boomarangs are shown, and are placed together, as one, to show their identical size. Then the magician stretches the rear boomerang by pulling it out a little. He then places the two shapes on the table, and one is seen to be quite clearly smaller than the other. The large boomerang is placed behind the other, and pushed, until they are again identical in size.

You can easily make a pair of these magic boomerangs from cardboard (see Diagram 1). You can draw or paint designs upon them. Apart from the 'funny noses' already mentioned, sets of this illusion have been made in the form of bananas and were

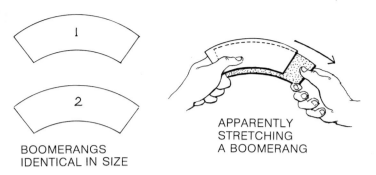

BOOMERANGS
IDENTICAL IN SIZE

APPARENTLY
STRETCHING
A BOOMERANG

issued, back in the thirties, as an advertising novelty.

As for the real boomerang, the kind used by the Aborigines of Australia: if it always comes back, how do you ever get rid of an old boomerang when you get a new one? Seriously though, as comedians always say, anthropologists assure us that the present-day Aborigines would not have been capable of inventing such a sophisticated weapon. So the puzzle is, were they once far smarter, or did they inherit it from some unknown civilisation?

Chapter 8
Making a start in magic

Any reader who is at all serious about adopting magic as a hobby will need to consider many things. In this volume we have tried to collect together and present for you a number of tricks which are suitable for the beginner. They are simple to understand and to perform, and of course have been selected for that reason. Needless to say, you may in due course wish to enlarge your knowledge and your magical repertoire. With this in mind, a visit to a magic shop would provide you with much additional material. For not only will you be able to purchase magical effects, complete with instructions and all the apparatus required, but also to make a selection from a great many books on tricks to be performed with everyday objects. There have been many thousands of books on magic, since the appearance of Hoffmann's *Modern Magic* in 1875, but only a small percentage of these are suitable for the beginner. For this reason, be sure to tell the magical salesman that you are just starting out in magic, so that he can recommend the right books for you. The people in such establishments are usually very helpful and more than willing to advise.

Having made a start by learning some simple tricks, you will of course wish to progress to the handling of tricks which require sleight of hand. Here again the same sources will provide a wealth of material, general and specialised. (You might wish to specialise in tricks with coins, cards, balls or thimbles. You will be able to find magical literature to cover all these subjects.)

Of course sleight of hand is very demanding and will require a great deal of practice if you are to become proficient. The simple tricks described in this book will also need practice. They might be easy enough to do, but to present them as they should be is something needing much practice. You need to be

Fig. 38. Painting of a typical box of tricks (1938). It is often a present of a box of tricks that starts a young person on the road to becoming a professional magician.

able to go through the motions of performing the trick, without having to think about it too much, if you are to be able to concentrate upon making it entertaining. Remember that to be able to entertain your audience is the most important aspect of all. A magic trick is not a puzzle . . . although all too often it is wrongly presented as such.

When you have presented your trick, what will happen? If it has been well done, your spectators should be not only mystified, but intrigued. However, the beginner often makes the mistake at this stage of allowing a sort of inquest to take place. One of the beholders will start this off by commencing a sort of logical breakdown of events. This can be dangerous, but how can you prevent this from happening? You can do so in two ways: first, if you entertain with the trick, even the most logical mind may not wish to dissect what you have done; second, a fresh trick! When you have finished your last trick, accept their compliments but make it clear that you do not wish to enter into an investigation. You could make a remark like, 'I don't like to question the magic, but just to enjoy it, as I hope you have!' Then change the subject, or even walk away from the group you have been entertaining. Excuses to do this can always be found, without causing offence.

This brings me to an important point, for, by behaving as indicated, you will be imposing a certain amount of control over your audience. This is very important, because no entertainer can survive as such if he cannot control the audience, at least minimally. If someone makes to pick up the pack of cards, at a moment when it would be inconvenient for him to do so, just make it clear that he should not do this. Don't snap at him, whatever you do. Rather say, 'Please, no distractions, I want to concentrate.' If you commence by explaining that your tricks are simple ones, and that you are not trying to compete with professional entertainers, your only wish being to amuse, most people will behave as they should, being happy that you are taking such trouble for their entertainment. But just now and then you will encounter the party bore or smart-alec type of person, who will delight in trying to spoil your little show. These people sometimes even try to bother professionals, who usually turn the tables on them nicely. But you, perhaps as a guest, cannot be too dominant in handling such a situation. Therefore you can only smile, and try to appeal to his better nature. Remember, most people will be on your side. Try saying, 'Yes, I appreciate that you know all about it, but don't you think you could be spoiling it for the others?' This can work in two ways. He may think better of his behaviour, and the other members of the audience may control him for you. (Nothing spurs people to action, like the hint that they may be cheated of something, in this case entertainment.)

There are only a few golden rules. The first of these is to remember that the normal rules of good and polite behaviour still apply to you, even if you are presenting a conjuring show. The second, never repeat a trick for the same audience, no matter how they may plead with you to do so. If you fall into this trap you will give them a second chance to spot how you do it. Remember, the second time they know what is going to happen, and so will know what to watch for. The third rule is never to tell your spectators how you do any of your tricks. The secrets of magic are ours to use, but not to betray.

Keep your performance lively and brief. Far better to have an audience eager for more when you have finished. Three or four tricks, if you are performing impromptu at a party, would be enough. You know, one of the world's greatest magicians, David Devant, had a repertoire of only eight tricks: and he did not perform all of these at any one time. How many tricks should you learn? Well, I think Devant's eight is a good number. Six would be enough. Remember that the less tricks you learn to perform, the more perfect can be your performance of them.

You may wish to present tricks at a spanking pace, or you may wish to be more deliberate. This matter of tempo is dictated to some extent by your own personality. It is important not to try to change your normal manner when you perform. Robert-Houdin once said: 'A magician is an actor, playing the part of a magician.' This is as it should be for the theatre or night-club conjurer, who works to people who do not know him as a person. But if you are among friends, you will not be expected to cease to be James or Sue or Bob, just because you are showing a few tricks.

The most important aspect of all is that you enjoy your own performances. Learn your tricks, perform them as well as you possibly can, and above all, don't worry too much. Worry is contagious, and so is joy and happiness. Far too many magicians tend to forget that it is the creation of joy and pleasure rather than puzzled bewilderment that should be their goal.

Always remember that phrase which George Bernard Shaw used, when commenting on a performance by Murray, 'I find the man more interesting than the trick.' The man, woman, boy or girl who presents a magic show must, in order to be a success, be more interesting than even the tricks themselves.

Just a purely technical point: wherever in the instructions for tricks in this book we refer to right or left hand, we are explaining as if to a right-handed person. This is because the greater number of readers will be right-handed. But left-handed readers have only to transpose the words left and right. Some of the greatest magicians have been left-handed, and it is no disadvantage magically. Indeed, as far as the handling of objects is concerned, the conjurer usually becomes truly ambidextrous.

The 'Svengali Pack'

Investigation of the literature available from your favourite magic shop will reveal a wealth of material with everything illustrated by photographs of the moves and sleights being performed. This is standard now, but it only became so in 1908 with Burling Hull, a young magician who revolutionised magical books by the use of photographs. He was a very inventive man, the self-styled 'Edison of Magic'. Like most innovators he made many enemies, and one of these referred to him in print as 'Hurling Bull'. Until 1940 Hull produced a great many booklets for conjurers with much original material. Publishers and those to whom he wrote letters, always remembered that he typed everything in capitals. They thought he did this for the effect that it created. Actually, Burling had bought an ex-post-office typewriter of the kind that was used for telegrams. This would only type capital letters.

In 1910 Hull invented a special pack of cards, which would enable a conjurer to 'force' a card on a spectator. This was very clever, but Hull did not quite realise what he had invented. Later, under the name of the 'Svengali Pack' it was exploited and sold by others. One of the very finest of those who performed with the pack was Joe Stuthard, a Canadian who demonstrated it in British stores in the late forties. With this pack, Joe could show that all the cards were different from each other, yet instantly find a freely selected card. In addition he could perform some twenty other tricks, all depending for their performance on the way in which the pack was constructed, rather than the sleight of hand. The cards could be made to change their faces, so that every card in the pack became the chosen card, and then to change their faces back to their normal aspects. The cards could be laid in a circle, and a table knife spun like a pointer to stop pointing to the chosen card. A card, chosen and held down upon the table by a spectator, would appear to change whilst still being held. The 'Svengali Pack' in fact did everything except sit up and beg.

Almost every professional magician in Britain has sold and demonstrated the 'Svengali Pack' in a store at some time or other. (For magic, as a profession, is not the most financially steady occupation.) I remember back in the sixties, when I was demonstrating the pack in a Blackpool store, hearing that Nelson Holt, who I knew to be one of the greatest of 'Svengali' workers, was demonstrating it on the North Pier. One evening I walked down to the pier to watch Nelson work. He was in the middle of his pitch, surrounded by a crowd of people who hung upon his every word. I should perhaps explain that Nelson was at that time an elderly man, with a mane of snow-white hair and a fiercely upturned moustache, very much the stage army colonel. He spoke with cultured tones, and those who bought the cards from him really felt that they were fortunate to be allowed to do so. He looked up from his labours, caught my eye, stroked his moustache and said: 'Dear boy, let us go for a spot of the old sarsaparilla!' I was worried when he left his cards, money, instruction sheets, and audience, to escort me to the pier bar. Fifteen minutes and three double Scotches later, he decided to return to his pitch. When we got there, the people he had left were still waiting to see the rest of his demonstration. They had not touched his cards, his instructions or his money!

But Nelson's liking for the 'old sarsaparilla' was to lead to his downfall. He lost his pitch on the pier, and had no place to work. Another Blackpool demonstrator, Big Stan, had a first-class pitch, but nothing to sell. So they got together, the idea being that Stan would 'pull a crowd' by telling the tale (which he did well) and then Nelson would take over. Well, Stan really let his imagination run riot, saying: 'I'm going to introduce you to a man what 'as come all the way from Las Vegas, what is in the United States of America, where 'ee 'as been banned from all the casinos on account that he always wins! This man will show you how you can win every time with 'is marvellous pack of cards!' Stan glanced round, to assure himself that Nelson was ready, and found to his horror that he was not there. Nelson had taken himself off for a spot of the old sarsparilla. Now Stan had worked hard to attract such a large crowd and did not wish to lose them. He had no idea how the 'Svengali' worked, but tried to squint at the instructions while still talking. The crowd, intrigued by his speech, were starting to become restless with the lack of action. Then, suddenly, unsteadily, but to Stan's great relief, Nelson reappeared. Stan bundled Nelson onto the little platform and hastily filled him in on what he had said. 'I've told 'em that you're a Yank, and you're going to show 'em how to win at cards!' Nelson nodded, in dismay, and addressed the crowd in his usual faultless English, saying: 'Gee-whizz, are you guys going to win a lot of dough!' That was his concession to what had been said, whereupon he gave his usual demonstration.

If everyone who had ever sold 'Svengali Packs' had given Burling Hull a pound, he would have been a wealthy man when he died in 1982 at the age of ninety.

I can think of no better purchase for a beginner in magic than the 'Svengali'.

Reversed card

This trick is done with a normal pack of cards. The magician offers the cards, fanned, for selection of one card by a spectator. The card having been taken from the pack, the magician implores the spectator who chose it to be sure to remember the card. He then invites him to replace it in the pack. This done, the magician spreads the cards on the table, and the selected card is the only reversed card in the pack.

Preparation: Immediately prior to performing the trick, the magician secretly reverses the face card of the pack, so that it is a back rather than showing pips.

Performance: Taking care not to show the face of the pack, the magician fans the cards for selection. Any card can be taken from the pack, and the magician makes a great deal of imploring the spectator to remember his card and to show it to the other people. During this distraction, the magician can easily turn the pack over in his hand. This means that the cards are now face upward, except for the reversed face card, but their appearance is unaltered. The chosen card is pushed back into the pack by the spectator, somewhere near the middle, as directed and supervised by the magician. So the position now is that the chosen card is near the middle of the pack, but face down, with all other cards, except the face card, being face up. Before spreading the cards, to reveal the reversed selection, the magician has to again turn the pack over. But this is done quickly and naturally. The pack rests on the left palm. The magician points to the table with his right forefinger, to show where he will spread the cards. As he does this he turns the left hand over, preventing the cards from falling with his left fingers and thumb, and then spreads them in an even ribbon, across the table. The cards will all appear showing their backs, except for the chosen card which shows its face. There is of course another face-up card on the front of the pack. But the magician is careful, when he spreads the cards, for this one not to show. The reversed, chosen card is pulled out of the pack for verification. The pack is picked up and cut a few times to lose the other reversed card.

Of course if the reversed card on the face is an ace (and you can as easily arrange for it to be that card as any other) you can repeat the spread, saying, 'Pity you can't do that with aces!' (The cutting of the pack will have brought the reversed ace near the centre.) This is one of those rare occasions when the repeating of a trick not only enhances it, but 'destroys the evidence'!

A quick trick, but a showy one, always admired when performed.

Chapter 9
Illusion and television

It is hardly surprising that Great Britain had the world's first regular television service, for it was the brain-child of the British inventor, Logie Baird. Those flickering images on a nine-inch screen may seem a bit of a joke now, but in the mid thirties they seemed like a miracle. Yes, and a miracle it was, to be able to watch a live performance from the Alexandra Palace in your drawing-room thirty miles away: even if it did seem as if you were viewing it through a bowl of jelly! Transmissions were suspended during World War II, but in the late 1940s television really started to be taken seriously.

As far as magic and illusion was concerned the established wonder-workers of course got an airing, but television started to create magical stars of its own. Among the first magicians to benefit and extend their careers through TV were Robert Harbin, Tommy Cooper and David Nixon.

Harbin, who had arrived in Britain twenty years earlier billed as 'The Boy Wizard From Sunny South Africa', had served an apprenticeship at Maskelyne's Theatre, and was already an experienced and inventive performer. He not only produced for the television audience a bewildering array of original disappearances, productions, transpositions and levitations, but popularised the art of Origami, Japanese paper-folding. His real name was Ned Williams, and he was a very charming, talented, but somewhat absent-minded man. I remember on one occasion encountering him in Davenport's magic shop, and thinking that he looked somewhat preoccupied. For some time he continued to glance at the magical apparatus on view, with a worried frown upon his face. Then, quite suddenly he turned to me and said: 'Dear boy, when I came in here, did I have a little dog with me?' I replied, 'No, Mr Harbin, I don't think so!' He looked even more worried, and said: 'I must have left it at Goldston's magic shop!'

Of course Tommy Cooper was a tower of strength to early television entertainment. So effective were his deliberate bunglings of a variety of tricks and illusions that the critics branded him 'a natural clown'. This was only partially true. Certainly the talent to be droll must have been there: but Tommy worked harder at perfecting his act than any other performer I ever knew. And a lot of that so-called 'gift' was the result of years of performing experience, in countless Empires, Palaces and Hippodromes. His infectious laugh, nervous mannerisms and a seeming inability to perform correctly the simplest of tricks endeared him to millions. Offstage Tommy was wonderful company and always a pleasure to be with. He would buy a trick at Davenport's, and would then say to me: 'Time for a cup of tea, boy!' (All his male friends were addressed as 'boy' – I think this had something to do with his Welsh ancestry!) We would then retreat to Lyon's, where he would convulse the waitresses with his attempts to make his newly purchased miracle work.

One night Tommy came to a theatre where I was performing, to watch me work. Afterwards he said, 'Who writes your material, boy?' When I told him it was all my own work he said, 'Write something for me. . . .' It was the start of a long association. Throughout his long reign as the Clown Prince of Magic, Tommy could always reduce me to tears of laughter with his inspired fooling. His early death has robbed the world of illusion of its own comic genius.

As for David Nixon, he gained his early experience by working as a member of a famous concert-party, the Fol-de-Rols. David was quite different from the usual, run-of-the-mill conjurer. He had a disarmingly apologetic manner, and was a most accomplished magician. Yet, curiously, it was as a member of a panel-game team that he first gained success on television. As a regular *What's my line?* teamster, he became very popular with viewers. Then, when the top people in television discovered that he also had a first-class speciality, they used his talents extensively. For many years, to the average viewer, David Nixon was *the* television magician.

During the early years of television the variety theatres had only benefited from their stars reaching a wider audience. With only one channel showing programmes for only two or three hours a night, the new medium hardly reduced their audiences. Unlike vaudeville in America, variety had survived the novelties of radio, and talking pictures, and seemed set to survive the competition of television. But with the introduction of commercial television in 1955, increased viewing time and more and better programmes, the picture began to change. The theatre-owners and managers made a number of mistakes at this point, which probably did more to hasten variety's end than television itself. Instead of taking advantage of the fact that they could still offer aspects of entertainment impossible on television at that time (colour, spectacle and the unique experience of sharing an entertainment with several hundred other people), they made the terrible error of cutting their costs, and offering their patrons less rather than more for their money. Moreover, the managements were beginning to realise that their theatres occupied very valuable sites, which chain-stores and other businesses wanted. So panic and greed contributed quite as much to the end of variety as did television.

But it was not only the several thousand people who had been regularly engaged as variety artistes who suffered. Television itself was the poorer, for it no longer had its training ground for light entertainment talent. An artist cannot learn his business on television, which is merely a showcase for a finished product. This meant that no new acts were arriving, and many established artistes left show business, because they could not be expected to exist on one or two appearances a year on the small screen.

The sixties was a lean period for magic, with both of the channels having to rely entirely on already established star magicians who could comfortably survive through a series. If one of the television shows wanted to screen a magical act new to viewers, they would have to import one from abroad.

But the seventies brought not only two extra channels and greatly extended viewing hours, plus colour, but also a fresh talent nursery in the form of a great rebirth in live entertainment via clubs, cabaret and cruise entertainments. Toward the end of the decade, much of this new talent had started to mature and the new wave of magicians started to arrive: Paul Daniels, Alan Shaxon, John Wade, Wayne Dobson and others had been waiting in the wings for the revival of interest in magic and illusion which now began.

The showing in the mid-seventies of television 'spectaculars' featuring a young Canadian illusionist, Doug Henning, really opened the flood-gates. The importation of his shows illustrated to British viewers that magic could be fast, exciting and intriguing. Younger viewers who had never been to the theatre were amazed and vastly entertained by Henning's presentations of great classic illusions. He carried it all off with an infectious enthusiasm and charm, illustrating to the new audience that illusion did not have to be anything like the boring performances at school shows. With shoulder-length hair and flower-power clothes, Henning transported them into a world of colour and sunshine, where anything could happen. He made a path for others to follow.

That path has been well trodden since by another young illusionist, David Copperfield, dynamic duo Siegfried and Roy, and the son of one of magic's all-time greats, Harry Blackstone Junior.

David Copperfield, still in his twenties, has assurance and charm, plus a great ability to use his expressive eyes effectively. Reminiscent of a younger Dante, he dresses his illusions to form sketches and playlets with a balletic touch. Instead of making a lady vanish for no good reason, he does so as part of the action in a drama, usually with a nostalgic appeal. The spectaculars featuring Siegfried and Roy have mostly been filmed in their actual locations in Las Vegas, where the duo have long been a popular cabaret attraction. They specialise in grand illusions with large animals, elephants, tigers, lions, leopards, jaguars, and their famous 'lepjag' (the result of their leopard and jaguar being kept as a pair)! Roy is an animal trainer as well as being a magician, which explains, in part at least, their playful handling of fierce jungle creatures. And where other magicians produce doves from silk squares, Siegfried and Roy produce flamingos!

In quite a different category is Harry Blackstone Junior. He has the deportment and command of an ex-army officer, which indeed he is. When Harry tells a spectator to do something, he does it! Apart from his big illusions, some of which he inherited from his famous father, he presents a number of small magical

Fig. 39. **David Copperfield** – a brilliant young magician from the USA, whose illusions include disappearing acts with a seven-ton jet and the Statue of Liberty.

Fig. 40. A poster of **Siegfried and Roy** – the outstanding American illusionists who use a variety of animals in their act, including lions and tigers.

effects with great style and skill. One of these, the 'Vanishing Bird-Cage', he effects while members of the audience hold the small, square cage. Harry recently ran a season on Broadway in New York, the first magic show to play there for many years. It was a wonderful show, quite as spectacular as anything that any of the greats of the golden era presented. I understand that the season grossed three million dollars at the box-office, but that Harry spent two and three-quarter millions in staging it! A great lesson for everyone in the theatre: give the people *more* than their moneysworth, and you will have a success.

What of Britain's new wave magic stars? Well, I suppose the first of these was the dynamic Paul Daniels, who emerged as a television star in the mid-seventies following a long club and cabaret apprenticeship. Paul has everything going for him. Quite apart from his obvious skill with sleight of hand, he has a great sense of theatre, and an unrivalled mental file of funny lines. If you step up on the stage to assist Paul he will first ask you your name. No matter how obscure your name may be, Paul will have a funny line to compliment it. If you are wearing a tweed jacket or a heliotrope dress, he will manage to find something amusing to say about your attire. It's all a glorious mixture of experience and sheer impromptu invention. No matter how cheeky his comments may be, you will not be offended, due to his pixie-like charm. Just as Blackstone repopularised magic on Broadway, so Paul reintroduced it as a form of entertainment in London's West End. When Paul took his show to the Prince of Wales Theatre in 1981, it was as an experiment, expected even by himself to run only a few weeks. But his name stayed over the theatre façade for more than eighteen months, a West End record for a magician. (Horace Goldin ran for sixteen weeks at the Palace in 1901, and Cecil Lyle's *Cavalcade of Mystery* ran for twenty-six weeks at the Aldwich in 1942, blitz or no blitz!) To see Paul on television is always a pleasure, but to see him in person is an experience.

As we go to press, that fine young British magician Johnny Hart is about to commence a season at London's Cambridge Theatre. This promises to be a fine production with spectacular illusions and scenic wonders. Johnny is known to us in Britain as the winner of the Magic Circle's first Young Magician of the Year contest. His wonderful manipulations, with cards and productions of parakeets and doves, have been a feature on television in several continents since then. Now he is an illusionist, and from all accounts a very fine one.

The wheel has turned full circle, with magic and illusion again becoming a popular and highly commercial form of entertainment. This is illustrated by the peak-hour showing of the popular series *Illusions*, which complements this book.

Chapter 10
Magic clubs, circles and properties

Most people have heard of the Magic Circle, even if they have only the vaguest idea of its function. A happy choice of title, for while there are dozens of other magical clubs and societies in Great Britain, the Magic Circle is the only one that seems to mean anything to the public. It is of course a splendid and important organisation in the world of magic. It has a fat rulebook, but its aims and code can be condensed into a few words. Its aim is to elevate the art of magic and preserve its secrets. The Circle meets on almost every Monday evening of the year at its Chenie Mews clubroom, just off London's Tottenham Court Road. There in the splendid miniature theatre, members are

Fig. 41. **Col Ling Soo** (Herbert J. Collings) – one of the founders of the Magic Circle in London.

treated to lectures and demonstrations on important aspects of their art. Although not intended to be a club for magical beginners, the Circle does offer associate-membership to the tyro in return for a promise of secrecy. Later, the associate can be 'auditioned' by a panel of experts, who will decide if he is worthy of becoming a full member. Of course, not all magical enthusiasts are performers or ever likely to be. So the Circle offers to such people the alternative of a written examination. Either way, it is ensured that only those with some knowledge and dedication are admitted to full membership. I have dealt with the system employed by the Magic Circle at some length, because it is similar to that followed by other magicians' societies.

A smaller but extremely vigorous magical organisation is the London Society of Magicians. Established in 1941, this Society held meetings throughout World War II, when other London clubs, including the Circle, felt it wiser to suspend activities. They met, every Friday, regardless of the blitz, in a cellar attached to a night-club called Pluto's, owned by one of the members, Knox Creighton. The address was $7\frac{1}{2}$ Thayer Street, an unlikely one for anything less unusual than a conjurers' club! Naturally, with so little competition, the Society gained a very high number of members. But with the return of peace and the resumption by other, more splendid organisations, the club went into a decline. However, like magic itself, the London Society has enjoyed a recent rebirth, and now flourishes, with meetings every second Friday at the studio attached to Davenports magic shop. As with the Circle, membership is open to all who are interested in magic, and can pass an audition, assuming that they are eighteen years of age or more. As with most modern magic clubs, the London Society accepts lady members. A notable exception to this rule is the Magic Circle, that august body who still consider that a female wizard is a witch!

Britain's second city boasts the longest-established magic club, the British Magical Society of Birmingham. Their aims, rules and activities follow the general trend, and they have one of the finest magical lecture-theatres in the country.

There are magicians' clubs in Manchester, Newcastle upon Tyne, Edinburgh, Glasgow, Leeds, Blackpool, Brighton,

Dover, and in dozens of other towns and cities throughout Great Britain: enquiry at your local town hall should supply you with an organisation that is near to where you live.

The International Brotherhood of Magicians is a world-wide organisation, with 'rings' all over the world. There is a British ring, with a membership of just under a thousand. They hold a convention each autumn, at a variety of resorts, north, south, east and west, in fairness to their far-flung membership.

A typical magician's convention will feature a gala show presenting the cream of professional wonder-workers from all over the world. In addition it will have a dealer's fair, where magical dealers can set up shop under one roof, to show their goods, demonstrate, sell their wares to the delegates, and squabble with each other. There are magical cabaret shows at the headquarters hotel, lectures, dinners and activities for non-magical wives and friends. Many magicians now make a convention part of their annual holiday. Great fun and not to be missed by any aspiring magi!

Most magic clubs are surprisingly dignified, but I have encountered exceptions. One club in East London had a most amazing array of official jewels worn at the meetings by the committee members. Even the humble members wore fezzes and red sashes! Each official had a title. The lady secretary was the Grand Secretarial Witch and the president was the Grand Supreme Wizard. (And to think that I had known them since they were Fred and Selina Willis!)

If you are genuinely interested in magic, are willing to respect its precious secrets, and can convince the Committee of this, you can become a member of your local magic club, or even the famous Magic Circle. You will have everything to gain and nothing to lose, except your yearly subscription, which is very modest in most cases. Magicians are for the most part a friendly crowd, and they will welcome a fresh face and a fresh audience for their pet tricks. Just a couple of warnings: if you are a beginner, do not try to kid your fellow members otherwise. Also, when one of them shows you a trick, never, never ask him to tell you how it is done. If it is one of his cherished secrets, a refusal will embarrass both of you. There are certain basic principles which any member will be glad to help you with, but an original trick is something else. After all, you are both there for the mutual enjoyment of a common interest. It is not a magician's job to teach others anything.

This brings me to the subject of tuition. You may feel that you will make a short cut by receiving tuition in the basics of magic, rather than gradually absorbing them. In which case, if you reside in London, you will be able to enroll for the classes organised by Davenport's magic shop, held in the lecture-theatre attached to their premises. Individual tuition, production and help for the would-be professional can be gained from one or two experts who advertise in *Abracadabra*, which is the world's only weekly magical magazine. You can order this through your magic shop, but it is not available through newsagents for reasons of secrecy. You can subscribe to the magazine, so that a copy will arrive on your doormat each Saturday morning. For subscription details, write to *Abracadabra*, Arden Forest Industrial Estate, Alcester, Warwickshire. Enclose a stamp for their reply.

Most of the magical societies publish their own magical magazines, which can vary from a duplicated monthly information sheet to a glossy production. The *Magic Circular* of the London Magic Circle, comes into the latter category. But apart from these and the weekly *Abracadabra* there are not many magic magazines. There are two published in the United States, *The Genii* and the *Magic Manuscript*. Copies of these can be obtained from most magic dealers, but of course they are received here rather later than published. Lastly, there are a few magazines produced especially for those interested in sleight of hand, with names like *Talon*, *Spellbinder*, and for the mentalist there is Peter Warlock's *Pentagram*.

One of the greatest joys for the beginner in magic is the perusal of the magical dealer's catalogue. From the several-hundred-page giants of firms like Davenport's down to the duplicated lists of small dealers, they are packed with sheer enjoyment. What fun to read each effect and try to figure out the method. These volumes are full of exciting phrases like: 'Positively no wires, threads or strings . . . yet it floats!' 'It' can of course be anything from a single playing-card to a huge, heavy metal globe. Your selection of goods from magical catalogues should be made very carefully, as due to the secrets involved the goods cannot possibly be exchanged. (Otherwise

Fig. 42. Inside Davenport's Magic Shop in London today – a typical magic store in that all the employees are magicians.

Fig. 43. Outside Davenport's Magic Shop and Studio in the Strand.

the customer might keep swapping one trick for another in order to learn as many secrets as possible!)

Secrecy over tricks and apparatus is preserved as much as possible. For centuries, magic was a closed shop, the secrets being passed only from father to son and master to apprentice. When a conjurer required a piece of apparatus, he would make a cardboard pattern, and enlist the services of local tinsmiths and carpenters. If a piece of metal apparatus was in two parts, each would be entrusted to a different tinsmith. But it was only a matter of time before an enterprising conjurer opened a business to supply his fellow wonder-workers. Towards the end of the eighteenth century such a supply house was opened in the Strand, by one Joseph Bland. His business was eventually incorporated into the toy emporium of Hamley's, and the

Fig. 44. A rare box of magic tricks dated 1895 from Hamley's in Regent Street. It was the Hamley's store that inspired the fifteen-year-old Lewis Davenport to start his own magic shop in 1898. *From the Davenport Collection.*

Regent Street store of that name includes a conjuring department to this day.

Another famous London store, Gamage's of Holborn, opened a magical department in the 1890s, and through the years a great many conjurers, later to become famous, worked behind their counters as magical demonstrators, such as V. R. Pitchford who became Cardini. A heavy smoker, he found a way to defy the store's non-smoking ban on its staff by frequently demonstrating a trick known as the 'Smoke-vase'. In this trick he would show a glass vase to be empty, place a lid of glass upon it, and cover it with a handkerchief. He would then light a cigarette, and fan the smoke towards the shrouded vase. When the handkerchief was removed, the vase would be found to be filled with smoke. Pitchford would manage to prolong that part of the trick where he was required to smoke the cigarette! When Robert Harbin arrived from South Africa in 1928, the only engagement he could secure was behind Gamage's counter, and as in Cardini's case it led to better things.

Gamage's most famous manager of things magical was Will Goldston, who used his position there as a stepping-stone to opening Will Goldston Ltd in Irving Street, just off Leicester Square. There, from 1913 to 1948, his little first-floor showroom became the mecca for magicians visiting London. His customers included Chung Ling Soo, Carl Hertz, Horace Goldin, Arnold de Biere and Houdini. When the latter was present, Goldston would flick a switch to ignite a small bulb at the entrance to his premises. This was a prearranged warning to certain of Houdini's rivals, who wished to avoid confrontation.

During the twenties and thirties a number of smaller, specialist dealers in apparatus appeared, selling mainly through the magical magazines, and quite unknown to the public. These included Edward Bagshawe, James Grayson, Henri Renaud, and Eric C. Lewis who now resides in California, designing and building illusions for Doug Henning and the David Copperfield spectaculars.

Between the two world wars a great many magical dealers were operating on the continent, and especially in Germany where the houses of Bartl, and J. F. Conradi were producing wonderful metal apparatus, and effects made of turned boxwood. In Paris, André Mayette ran a splendid magic shop on the city's left bank, where he would watch his shop from the table of the café opposite, as he sipped his absinthe. Another Parisian builder of apparatus was Guy Bert, who was, and is, a bit of a character. Wild-haired, wide-eyed and altogether charming, he always seemed to me to be the typical eccentric genius. I visited him once in company with Fred Kaps, a wonderful magician from Holland, with a wicked sense of humour. At that time, Guy was working on a wonderful growing tree, for the Folies Bergères. I should explain that once the tree had grown it took Guy half an hour to pack it all back in its vase. As we left, Fred flicked the switch to start the irreversible growing action, and then ran for his life.

In America, where mail order began, the leading dealer in the thirties was Percy Abbott, who started his business with a single trick called 'Squash'. In this, a glass of whisky melted away, between the conjurer's hands. Percy sold hundreds of them, and wanted to operate on a larger scale. He found a field in Colon, Michigan, erected some large tin sheds, and painted skeletons on their sides, and the caption 'Abbott Magic Com-

Fig. 45. An early set of wooden tricks from Germany dated 1910. *From the Davenport Collection.*

pany'. But before he could commence manufacturing he needed capital, so he approached a bank, who sent their representative to see his operation. Prior to the visit, Percy got some packing-cases and covered them with canvas sheets, and placed them in one of the sheds. He took the man from the bank in there, pointing grandly to the shrouded crates, saying that this was his 'plant', but that it was not in use at this time. He then led the way into the other shed, where he had seated every friend he could muster, dressed in overalls, and pretending to assemble pieces of apparatus from Percy's own act. The resulting loan enabled Abbott's to become one of the world's biggest magical supply houses!

Back in London, the long-established magical house of Lewis Davenport came into its own in the thirties, rapidly

Fig. 46. The four generations of Davenports – spanning over a hundred years of an unbroken line of professional magicians. The picture of Lewis is in the centre, the picture of his son George in the foreground, and his granddaughter, Betty, and great-grandsons, Fergus and Billy are in the family group.

growing to become the largest such enterprise in Europe, possibly in the world. Today they can be found in their magnificent new premises in the Charing Cross underpass, where they can supply anything from a tiny pocket trick to the biggest stage illusion. Their new complex includes a lecture-theatre and a school of magic. The House of Davenport retains the nostalgia and wonderment of other times, yet moves through modern technology towards the twenty-first century.

Chapter 11
Magic in the twenty-first century

In the television series *Illusions*, and in this book, we have traced the story of magic: its origins, history, personalities and illusions, from the witch-doctors to David Copperfield, and from a simple trick with a shell and pebble to Harbin's 'Zig-Zag Lady'. But as time speeds us toward the next century, we have reached the moment when great changes in lifestyles and entertainment patterns must begin to affect the magician's art.

The revolution started with the virtual disappearance of live theatre magic. The clubs and cabarets which replaced the theatres as a venue are now themselves in eclipse. Yet magic is more popular than ever, on television, and as a hobby soon to rival stamp-collecting or fishing. Television, both the established and cable variety, has brought the magician into millions of homes. Yet these viewing patterns themselves may be altered by the emergence of the home computer. Millions of people now spend a great deal of that viewing time, watching and participating in computer-entertainment. They no longer play games with playing-cards or chessmen, but sit and control symbols of these on a screen. Twenty years from now, if a magician offers them a pack of cards for selection, will they recognise those objects; indeed, will the magician be able to obtain such a thing as a pack of playing-cards? Oh yes, and how about that classic trick, the production of a white rabbit from a top-hat? Even now a conjurer at a party has to explain the top hat, which has long ceased to be an everyday object. The white rabbit is still understood, but how long will this be so? The keeping of rabbits as domestic pets may cease with the increasing obsession with hygiene; wild rabbits may disappear through the loss of their environment. Surely though there will be plenty of other tricks for the future's audiences to enjoy, such as the production of a delicious cake from a seemingly empty cakepan, to be divided and enjoyed by the children. Well, perhaps they won't recognise a cake as, we are told, the population of the vastly overcrowded world will have to survive on vitamin tablets. The production of a live dove from a handkerchief is out too. Handkerchiefs, already largely replaced by paper tissues, will be out of the question. As for mind-reading tricks, thought-transference will be a regular school subject, along with metal-bending by mental effort.

But perhaps I am painting a gloomy picture of the future of the world in general and illusion in particular. It may well be that the environmentalists will save the flora and fauna of our planet, and that people will start to realise that the character-forming advantages of keeping pets by far outweigh the hygienic disadvantages. Indeed, it is even possible for the wheel to turn full circle, and for people to realise that television is not a substitute for real-live entertainment: the two forms can complement each other, as can a book and a television series.

When I was ten years old I encountered the famous Horace Goldin in Davenport's magic shop. He wore a vast, fur-trimmed overcoat, from beneath the collar of which peeped the tiniest black dog I had ever seen. He spoke with a stammer and a heavy Polish accent, but he swallowed a penknife, and produced several silver coins from my left ear. Then he winked at me, waved to George Davenport, and made an exit. Kindly George explained: 'That was Horace Goldin!' But I already knew, having seen Goldin on the stage, and did I not have one of his discarded posters pinned on the wall of my room?

The future of illusion is assured just so long as a star-magician will take the trouble to swallow a penknife for a small boy.

Epilogue

Our story is over and Val Andrews and I hope you have enjoyed this brief glimpse into the story of magic to make you consider trying to mystify your friends with some of the tricks discussed within these pages.

We have suggested how you could start magic as a hobby and by offering a number of tricks after each chapter – nearly forty effects – we hope by now you have tried a few of them on your friends. Some we have deliberately not explained as an incentive for you to go out and find a magic shop and discover the wonders of it.

Do not be discouraged too much when you first perform if your tricks are found out. It simply means you have either not practised enough or have not practised properly. Every magician has a mirror at home and he will work in front of that until he can fool himself, so try the mirror test before performing any effect.

Next, try not to over-elaborate or milk a trick. Do it neatly, and to a routine you have rehearsed; then, when you have finished, just put it away in your pocket or wherever. If your audience have liked it pull out another and do it and so on. By audience we mean anyone who will watch you perform . . . don't be too proud to perform for anyone, especially close friends, for they will certainly tell you if you have done it well or badly.

We have tried in this book to advise you repeatedly that it is not the complexity of the actual trick mechanism that is important, it is the effect on the audience. Many magicians themselves fall into this trap. They are convinced that a trick has to be highly complicated and demanding years of practice before they should offer it as entertainment. The Americans had a wonderful axiom in business administration which was known as the KISS principle. Keep it Simple Stupid!

You may well have been impressed by the incredible careers of some of the magicians in this book. If you knew how they actually did the illusions and tricks they performed with enormous success you would be astounded how simple many of them are with regard to the mechanisms. What these great illusions had above all was flair, and it was this sense of theatre and drama that made them great. In any performance you give you must bring this sense of theatre into it or your audience will have no feel for the effect of the tricks. Try and act as much as you can. You will be surprised just how much an effect this has, not only on the audience but on your own enjoyment.

You will no doubt have been impressed by magicians such as Houdini, Horace Goldin and Chung Ling Soo. Their greatness lay in their ability to mix tricks and effects so that as far as the audience were concerned they were all mystifying. In fact some were extremely simple tricks, but certainly their own brilliance and inventive ability allowed them to perform extremely difficult tricks. However, we have used the word 'inventive' as this is the most important factor in any trick you learn. What you learn is one person's or the basic method of doing a trick. Don't think that that is the only way of doing it. You must now take that trick, practise it, and in practising it according to the instructions put your own interpretation on to it. You may totally change it. You may reverse the way it is done. It doesn't matter as long as it appears fresh to you and to your audience.

So, to recap, we have suggested to you that if you are interested in performing a trick you should think about approaching it in a logical sequence. First learn the trick thoroughly according to its difficulty. For you a particular trick may take three minutes to learn; to another it may take a week; or they may never ever be able to do it. This is the first important fact to understand. Some magicians pick up card tricks very easily, others cannot do a card trick to save their lives! By going over the tricks suggested in this book you will begin to appreciate which are for you and which are not. Learn tricks which are easy for you or which you can master quickly. Return to the more difficult ones later.

Now you have learned the trick, in front of a mirror, you now think about how you are going to perform it. The two processes are completely separate. You work on, say, the story you will tell or the way you will present it, or what inspiration or novelty your own imagination can bring to the trick or whatever. This is a critical phase and so often missed out. Let us repeat . . . the presentation of a trick is as important as the trick itself. Chung Ling Soo took as much care and attention over his dress and presentation as he did over the trick itself.

You now have learned the trick, you have worked on your own style of presentation and brought your own ideas into the trick. What next? Well, as already mentioned, you must now put this trick into some sensible order or sequence with another trick. Never ever have only one trick in your repertoire. Try another in the same logical sequence as above. You now have two tricks. Now you try and put the two together so that one follows the other in some logical order. Say your first trick is the 'Eerie Matchbox' at the end of Chapter One. Your next is say the 'Chinese Compass' at the end of Chapter Three. There is no logical connection between a rising matchbox and an odd effect with a compass. Well, think about it. Your story could start by saying that a thousand years ago there was a great Chinese magician by the name of Who Flung-Who, and this great wizard was asked by the Emperor of China, Long Tin-Can, to perform a feat of magic or else he would be burned at the stake. So Who Flung-Who asked to see the box of matches which the Emperor was going to use to light the fire and placed it on his hand like this . . . and lo and behold it rose to the amazement of all the court. The magician now asked the Emperor to ask the matchbox to rise and he did and lo and behold . . . the box rose to the Emperor's command.

While all this talk is going on you are of course performing the 'Eerie Matchbox' trick. You can do what you like with the story. To finish, you now say that the Emperor was so delighted with the magician that he offered the hand of his daughter in marriage if the magician could perform another miracle. So Who Flung-Who took out from his robes a simple card on which was an arrow. He said to the Emperor, 'Look, your Imperial Highness, whichever way I turn the compass it always points in the same direction'. You now move the compass about its axis, then swing it about between your hands as if undecided where to place it and of course select the second position which allows the arrow to point in the same direction when revolved.

You do the same again. 'However, you continue, 'should your enemies ever capture the compass, they will find it useless as whichever way they turn the compass it will point in the wrong direction'. As you say this you of course move the compass to a position which will now repeat itself when turned. You finish your story by saying that the Emperor was so pleased he gave his daughter to the magician and they all lived happily ever after.

So you see from what appeared to be a highly improbable linking of two tricks a simple story has bound the two together into an interesting presentation which will keep your audience's attention. It also finishes with your two tricks neatly. If you try this you will find it enormous fun. Certainly it is a hobby that overcomes language barriers and can be done in any company of any age. For the authors it has been not just the way we earn our living but our hobby and one in which families can join in and participate actively.

Magic is a living art, not a dead and buried thing of the past. If you are interested in trying to develop your skills then start today. Find your local magical society or dealer and if you do not have one in your locality then get in touch with us here at Davenport's and we will try to assist you. For those of you who need help there is a fully equipped studio and training school available so you need never be stuck for advice. We can be found in the Charing Cross Underground Shopping Arcade, Strand, London WC2N 4HZ.